OUT OF THE CALIFORNIA SWAMPS

COMING OF AGE AT THE END OF A GOLDEN ERA

Michael Engle

authorHOUSE

AuthorHouse™
1663 Liberty Drive
Bloomington, IN 47403
www.authorhouse.com
Phone: 833-262-8899

Published by AuthorHouse 10/19/2020

ISBN: 978-1-4490-1351-6 (sc)

Print information available on the last page.

This book is printed on acid-free paper.

A million words delineate the problem, one word —the solution.

try

A SEA OF REGRET is churning behind me
And I look forward upon a dark horizon
Why do I live?

A STAR IS BORN from the death of itself
A collapsing into itself that forms a black hole
Comparable to the center of the earth
And through the other side of this anti-matter
Emerges a new star
Born from a passageway through the gravitational pit
An abyss within the universe
A dungeon created by the heavens

Each of the three books of Dante's Comedy
Ends with the word "star"
And as the Inferno comes to a close
The two pilgrims arrive at the site
Where Dis is locked in time
At the bottom of the well
That encompasses every evil
A dungeon created by the heavens

And like the birth of a new star
The pilgrims make their way
Through the underside of the beast
Through a passageway underneath the eternal abyss
Emerging anew at the foot of a climb to life
Much the way I sought the bottom
In search of a passage home to the stars

A steep hill is yet before me
And slothfully I rest dreamingly on the slope
I'm where I need to be
And though I linger, I am caressed by the winds of hope

Above me gleams a golden dreamy future
With angels in the skies and tears of joy in our eyes
And all the anguish we were destined to endure
Fans a joyous flame that never dies

I've been flaking out on religious experiences
And faith without works is dead some wise one's say
But to whom am I to be made inferior hence?
For only Jesus was perfect each and everyday

How can you help but be a little crazy
When youth condemned you to a life of hunger
And you can will the change but I'm feeling lazy
And someone wants to pull me under

But despite my sins I possess a deep passion
And it manifests in magical and unpredictable ways
As it's a gift from our God of exemplary compassion
Who forgives our trespasses and endless delays

And at the foot of the climb
Where I set up camp years ago
We await an important time
When we finally know

A WILD NOVEMBER wind
Blew the sand into the footprints left behind
And so erased the remembrance of the bleeding summer
But also reveals how our time can be lost forever

Unless I can build a monument with my life
That will stand the test of time
The sands of the hourglass will cover every trace
And this life will forever be forgotten

An outcast like me has to rise above
And leave an indelible mark in time
A testament to greatness discarded by the tribe
And not merely a meaningless rhyme

And when I become exasperated
And feel as though they are trying to keep me down
I have to remind myself that I'm exhausted most
By overcoming my nagging and persistent deficiencies

But the wind can conceal that which came before
And wipe away the traces of our misdeeds
And fill in the holes of hatred and resentment
That lie in the sands I have traveled until now

And quite a desert it has been
Seemingly endless until the dawn
A conundrum of perpetual night
But the winds of change lead us on

Like Emily Dickinson describes
I behold an endless midnight it seems
With midnight in my past and grave night in my midst
And yet through the maelstrom I can imagine a new dawn

Like a straggler on a deserted platform
Alone and lost at sea, holding a lantern up to the unflinching darkness

So newly arrived from my eternal roost in nonexistence
That I don't know how to not have hope

And when the shrill winds blow in from the North
Though they chill me to the bone they also bring something else
A change, in the season and in the times
In myself and in the world of hurt, carried by the gusty winds of love

Ah the digital age
IPOD the size of a quarter
U2 comes through in a collection of bites
And Metallica is reluctant to embrace this new world

Around the time they became multi millionaires
There was a shift taking place
Analog becoming digitized
And nothing has been so spiritual since

The IPOD can only recreate the soul from the past
This new age suffers a distinctive lack
Old Metallica was a religious experience
And old U2 the same

But you just don't feel them anymore
One needs to FEEL their suffering
But the rich don't feel anything anymore
And thus the music is as bland as a preacher devoid of the Holy Spirit

Once money fills the gaps of one's suffering
And the soul ceases to yearn and burn
Jesus instructs them to give their money away
For it has put the heart to sleep

And oh yeah the digital age
It has created a vacuum as well
We are broken up and segmented as a society
Others are impediments and harmony is absent

We travel in cars, talk through computers
Don't talk to strangers, don't co-operate
Cel phones seal us off from one another ironically
We walk through the public square having a private conversation

Everything is broken up into bits and reconfigured
Even our religion

Bob Marley sounds flat through the digitization
And no one has any passion anymore

Isolation makes us numb
And we are so disconnected with everyone else
And in turn they're so disconnected from us
That compassion is eroded away

The digital age is full of partially downloaded hate
We blog our hateful views from our cells
We e mail them to people we haven't seen
And TV is a gauge to test the cultural waters

And everyone is so good looking now
Images created digitally on MySpace
A new age persona, constructed from the fragments
And rationality is king

But still everything is moderate
Even the fundamentalist radicals stand for something superficial these days
Terrorism is such a bread winner for George Bush
Because they are hidden in fragmented cells

A perfect bi-product of the digital age
A perfect symbol of the egregious separation
Analog come back, I don't care if it's more cumbersome for Ben Harper to record
Modernism is solidarity and unity, Post Modernism is a throwback to the dark ages

Entropy
The end of the spiral
The return
The Phoenix rising from its own ashes

ALL ENTERTAINERS ARE mere pawns of the devil
And ambition is an infernal wind
But Chris Rock thinks he's a hero
'Cuz he hangs with Oprah and Jim Carrey

But none shall change the world like me
And I don't have to do shit
And they will say I am poisoned with delusions of grandeur
But how can I when they all look down on me?

The stone that builder refused
I merely give it up to God
I don't aspire to be an actor
Reveling in hypothetical cookie cutter realities

Most of you can't hear me
And that's cool, because I no longer need to be popular
The worst are the leaders
Killing in the name of

Listen to your president, listen to Chris Rock
Remember the Anti Christ will be popular as fuck
I have God on my side
Did Jesus beg for Peter to be his friend?

He ended up denying him at the crucial moment
Frickin' Thomas needed proof even after he died
Most of you are stinkin' Judas's
Proclaiming allegiance only to betray

That's why I don't want to be liked by American's
The American way is to say fuck you all
We've been saying that from the start

England, Fuck you all
Confederacy, Fuck you all
Germany and Japan, fuck you all
Vietnam and Iraq, you know what I'm sayin'

But I rebel right from inside this mother fucker
I got my two Bachelors degrees biatch
I got my career
I'll be right here saying "Eat a big Dick, bitches"

All your superficiality
All your pretension
All your competition
All of your egotistical ambition

Yet none of you has anything to say
And I am so alone
But after thirty years of being an outcast
I now call it home

YEARS AND YEARS OF hurt have forged me
Into a loaded gun of spite
And yes Jesus said to forgive
But he will also come again on the stars

And he ain't gonna' look like Chris Christopherson in Blade
He's gonna' have a gnarly sword coming out of his mouth
And his words are gonna make all you godless bitches melt
Like the wicked witch of the East when Dorthy doused that nasty bitch with water

And like him I will be avenged
Not through any direct action of my own
But merely through the turning of the planet
My rise will not be denied

All of you cling to your favorite stars
Athletes, actors, perhaps bands and rappers
And you think these will rescue you from yourselves
But only I am an individual

I only let the river flow
And practice what I learned from the ancients
Surrender, give your burden to Jesus
Humbly go where the waters of time take you

Quit interfering so that your ego can be appeased
Quit ambitiously seeking acceptance on a large scale
Again the Anti Christ will be beloved world wide
And only bad-ass motherfuckers like myself will smell him a mile away

I'm so glad I stayed lonely, and never compromised so you all would have me
Pearl Jam's music doesn't mean shit anymore but they are more popular than ever
I'm not gonna' be a "Lost Cause" like Beck
I'm a "Man with a mission" like Greg Graffin

Only I believe in God
Not like the ambitious Christians

Selling Jesus and seeking your patronage
I believe alone in a room at night by myself

I am the partner of the down trodden
No one is below me
Only those who think themselves something else do I call bitches
If you think you're cool I am your arch rival

My time is coming around
Even if it is the end of the world
Despite my sex crimes and pot smoking
"This train is bound for GLORY"

ALL I CAN SAY FOR myself is that I am crushed by her burden
But at least I'm being crushed by her
Constant pain but then I'm punished for escaping
But it can't go on like this forever

Am I sick and tired enough?
Or will I need more convincing
So far my life's been tough
27 years and still sinning

The pain will arrive in time
Like clockwork and I'll decide
To alleviate or start my climb
And sum it all up in a futile rhyme

Beatrice has called on me
Jesus, God and Mary too
But I just can't take up this chore
Love and truth = black and blue

With the mud stains of hell
From which I was born
I'll begin to ascend from the well
With the memories of bitter scorn

Or will I, perhaps I'll put it off
Again like I have so often
Pick another day to stop
When the blow may be softened

Devote my life to this I must
Like Jesus to the cross
I must do what I'm told with no fuss
But I can't help but feel that all is lost

Darkness and despair are all I've known
Desperate now for the idea of my true home

AMERICANS ARE COMPLETELY preoccupied with fat
They have things low in carbs
Low in trans fat, whatever the fuck that means
People on the South Beach Diet
People on Jenny Crank
People listening to how Operah shed her whaledom
Dr. Phil, Martha Stuart, Weight Watchers
Fat free chips, low cal salads, Diet Coke
And yet obesity reigns supreme here in the land of the fat
Yet my Dad's father told him to eat the fat on his meat
Said it was good for him
And I've seen pictures of my dad as a kid
He was a pole, it's all in the mind
Lethargic people get fat
Lazy people get fat
Look at our culture
Everything has to be easy
We bitch about havin' to do laundry when all you do is put the shit in and push a button
Look at what ancient people had to do
Lazy Americans
Drive Thru, Drive up teller,
Order on-line, drive down the street
Watch TV as soon as you get home from your sit on your ass all day job
Or you see clones patting themselves on the back because they managed to stay thin
Jogging pretentiously down the strand
Basically resorting to that because their lives are so fuckin' easy
Billy Blanks Taebo
7 second abs
24 hour fitness
All to overcome the fat that is bulging out of us
So go ahead America
Continue to do your stupid shit
Label things low in carbs
Eat sugar free cookies and pretend to like the taste
Avoid potatoes like the plague
And you'll just get fatter and fatter and fatter
Pretty soon obesity will be so widely overlooked that a three hundred pound chick will be a model

Fat ass kooks will think she's hot
Fat will become accepted like Homosexuals are
Sickness will become the norm
All because we've lost our collective spirit in this country
Tending to a soul would keep you occupied with your bored asses
A conscience is the best fitness coach
Ask yourself this
Maybe I should go out and do something
Maybe I will walk since its right up the road
Maybe I've eaten enough
Maybe I'm only eating because I'm so miserable that the only joy I get out of life
Is doing just that to sate the yearning for inner peace that has been
Lacking since you can remember.
Maybe it's pleasure to escape the pain
I 'm not eating for nourishment anymore am I
No you're eating for the distraction
The same way a druggie shoots up
I feel so alone, but at least when I end up a "big 'ol pile of them bones", these bones will be
seen from the outside.

An entire lifetime of misery
I just don't get it!
I continuously consciously and knowingly
Head south and regret it

And if I can go this far south
And build upon regret
How many others will too come down
Into my home and native pit

AN ESSENTIAL TENET OF American culture is the quest to look down on others.
Wear the right clothes, drive the right car, and live in the right town
Do the right activities, make sure people are impressed with your outward appearance
And you can successfully assimilate which means you now have the right to condescend others
I have always been a rebel, because I choose to be honest
America has always hated me for that, I also care about people, you're not supposed to do that either
It's lonely work bein' a rebel with a cause

An interview with two collegiate athletes reveals
The truth about our education system
"Give this guy some propaganda."
One of them astutely remarks.
I was more articulate in fifth grade than this so called
College student.

But he was paid to go to school.
He probably won't even graduate but
He's given the opportunity.
He is paid to go to school,
Meanwhile I am sent through a bureaucratic runaround that seemed to have no end
As well as forced to pay an arm and a leg
And all I wanted to do was enhance my mind and
Follow my dreams of attending the misty school in the redwoods

But football gets ratings and ratings equals money
Thus the linebacker at SC, gets paid
I receive an education he never gets
I like to study philosophy, poetry and religion
I am a thinker
America sees no capitalistic benefit in someone like me
So I am on my own

Oh sure I got a little financial aid
Maybe a few handouts here and there
But I was reluctantly admitted
And it was a major pain in the ass to get through
Not because the curriculum was challenging
No the runaround, the paperwork, the economics was challenging
I wasn't popular, chicks dissed me as hard as the teachers did

Basically, because I don't play football,
Because I don't care about surfing and motor-cross
Because I am a thinker and a philosopher and not
A circus performer, America could give a fuck about me
Basically I don't have any capitalistic promise
Basically my body is denigrated
Basically it's me against the world

Another chance to escape befalls me
What can I do about my past?
What will be my fate this time?
And how long will this fragile state last?

Pathetic is my giving in
Old hat is my tired sin
But still I truly doubt my ability and will
And doubt that this time my climb truly begins.

ANOTHER NIGHT I WASHED upon the shore of nothingness
And retreated to a frenzy of drugs and masturbation
Another night of squandered hopes and ugliness
Another night of high hopes ends in frustration

Everybody hates me anymore, I'm the low man on the totem pole now
Wanted guys only dis me, they're the one's the hot chicks want
Whoever they want whatever creed or ethnicity allowed
I am undesirable and lonely, no matter what bars I haunt

My friends are good enough, my life is good enough
I'm merely a repulsive human being, with no self-esteem
I'm gonna' stop caring, despite myself
Just too many years of knowing I can't get clean

And not just clean off of drugs, we all know I need that
I mean clean as in slate, a new start, a time past my past
But it's all a lie now, right, the stories old and flat
With nothing left to lose, I retreat to God at last

Jesus I come to you now, because there ain't no chicks for me
And what if there were , I say goodbye with glee
I had another week long crush dissolve into the sea
And another beautiful girl I have to forget to be free

This torrent of emotions assails me every day
I'm rejected, I'm dismissed, and I'm always thrown away
I have to go be good, and follow what they told me
Or I'll die again and again in this familiar dismay

Another night of retreating from the staggering forces
Pushing down on my dreams and trying to merely
Stifle me out of existence so I don't threaten the course
The human race is progressing down drearily

More enlightened and competent than them
I'm met with grave opposition from the frightful

Who do what they have to do to bury this gem
Because in comparison they are not nearly as delightful

But my spirit cannot be defused by friend or foe
Even when there is no where on Earth for me to go
They will give me no shelter so my harvest can be sewn
Nor a fair wage because deep down they all know

That I am on my way to the chariot of glory
So God commands me to this desert to heal
The afflictions that assailed me early in my story
And learn compassion for those who hate and steal

God has known all along that I was on my way to him
And relentless was his love for me to only reach for it
The signs of his love are omnipresent despite my wretched sins
And forever smiling does he beckon me home from this dry pit

And as I lay down in this inferno somewhere between lost and found
And the nuts and bolts of the rational world still hold me to the ground
The messages that I read loud and clear in my soul are so profound
I somehow keep the faith knowing that I am coming around

And as for all those who assail me on purpose or despite themselves
I will treat as Jesus has commanded me to with love and justice
For even on the cross he forgave his executioners because they suffered in hell
I will not give in to hate and vindictiveness like the loveless

The reason we don't give in to hate and wish ills on others ever
Is because we will eventually be released from our bondage
And God forbid that in despair we clung to words like never
And allowed ourselves to believe that the light was absconded

God gives us this journey to learn of Him and His ways
And his holy spirit will always descend upon the faithful
There are bi products of free will such as death and disarray
But Jesus came and taught us to be graceful

So when you feel hatred emerging upon your lips
Stop and remind yourself that you will regret it if they fly out
And heed the teaching of our master Jesus and his wonderful tips
And you will forever be delivered from hatred, fear and doubt

Apologies apologies always from me
Humility turning to humiliated
Always accepting the blame
Always letting others use me as a scapegoat
But I'm not gonna' do it anymore

Being pushed around is not what God wished for me
This society trying to make me feel wrong
Acting like there is something definitely wrong with me
When there is something tragically wrong with all of you
And I'm not gonna' do it anymore

I'm gonna' hear some apologies from now on
They are gonna' bow down to me for a change
They are gonna' acquiesce to me
And sin is the secret and shame is the destroyer
And I'm not gonna' do it anymore

I have been awakened as if from a dream
I don't need to apologize for anything
My thoughts are as vital and valid as anyone's
More so in fact than most of the clones
And I won't cower to them anymore

Any result is better than humiliation
Humility is different than humiliation
Shame and guilt have made me hate myself
And self hate has made me cower to others
And I'm not gonna' do it anymore

I know the keys to my low self esteem
I know how I am raped each day
It's the way God has led me to repent
And the suffering was more agonizing than death
And I'm not gonna' do it anymore

My young mind was corrupted by filth
My habits became atrocious

And I loathed myself for carrying on with them
But these habits trace back to my early days
And I'm not gonna' do it anymore

I will be strong in the face of opposition
Those who desperately need to keep me down
Will learn that I am not going anywhere
And those who knew me in the past don't know me today
For I'm not who I was anymore

As a chapter comes to a close
And I emerge as a new creation
I reflect upon the path I chose
And wonder why there was ever any hesitation

Why was I so reluctant
To leave behind a filthy life
A message so redundant
That it carved my soul with a knife

Simply leave behind the old ways
And begin to see God's favor upon us
Follow your heart into this new day
And stop making such a fuss

As soon as I began this eternal climb
My life drastically improved
And instead of regretting all the wasted time
I must merely thank God that I finally made my move

Like Frederick Douglass I had to take
My opportunity to escape bondage and despair
And make my way North and leave only a wake
Upon which my captors can ponder and stare

We as humans strive though we stumble
But sometimes decisively we are called to Him
And we stand before Him humble
And how the light had been so dim

That led us on some dark nights
And love was merely a whisper tormenting
A soul deprived of sight
Stagnant and fermenting

But tonight I see clearly
And soberly I proceed
And I love God and Life dearly
And progress comes with God's speed

As I FIND MYSELF in the mood for oldies
And throw on some K-Earth 101
And I begin to place this music from the 50's and 60's
In it's cultural context
With the music that came before and the music that followed

This was the golden age of music
The people created a platform with which to create
Great music came out frequently
Music that stands the test of time
And the word underground still didn't pertain

Jump ahead forty or fifty years
And the music has been hijacked by the dead
The soulless took over the entire world
The TV, the movies, and of course our precious music
Everything good now gets destroyed, everything!!!

Don't let anyone tell you different
People wander through the world these days like corpses with a pulse
Good songs are about as frequent as solar eclipses
And the artists that perform them are extolled as gods
Ruining all that once could have been really cool

But not during the fifties and sixties
The music on the radio had soul and feeling
The people were alive and thriving
An artist had a shot
The parasites didn't control everything, not everything

I think of artists like Tool and Marilyn Manson
Like voices crying out in the wilderness
Like the last screams of integrity and soul
Like the dying of an age
Taking place before your tragic eyes

But the fifties and sixties shined
Diverse bands created soulful sounds
Numerous artists contributed to the strength of the culture
The people still had souls
America was still alive

As I was driving on the road one night
Traveling about fifty
With a line of cars approaching and behind
On the two lane street
The car ahead of me suddenly veered
Revealing a terrified coyote
In my headlights he stiffened and sneered
And made a face I'll never forget
Terrified, he braced himself to die
His back arched, his mouth smiled in fear
I slammed on my breaks and veered
And the oncoming traffic yielded to the beast
And he managed this time to get clear
I was shocked as I drove on
It didn't hit me for about thirty seconds or so
Then I moaned and wailed in pain
My heart was moved with pity for the scared beast
Our brother without a home
That man has evicted to the streets
It's just a matter time before the cars get him
Or perhaps starvation or worse
Maybe some white trash hick will shoot him
Maybe the pack has been disseminated
I became so very sad for him
So very, very sad
Why is this I wonder
True it is that I love the beasts of the world
True it is that I silently mourn the state of the world
But the look of that coyote in my headlights
Bracing himself for obliteration
That look was seared upon my consciousness
I realize that that look is how I am
That look is how I face the day
Vulnerable and trapped
Facing pending horror
To scared to think
To shocked to act
Just frozen and smiling

The smile of fear and terror
The smile of helplessness
And his life was spared for what?
To carry on in a dying world
Part of a dying breed
I realized that I am that coyote
I am in that exact predicament
And it's only a matter of time for me
And I've been scared stiff
Frozen in the headlights of doom
Smiling my fight or flight response
Since the day I was poisoned
When I was a child of five
Like the coyote still alive
Traumatized, despaired and forgotten
Tonight I managed to cross once more
Goodnight beast and God bless you and I

Be still my exasperated mind
Processing all of this devastating data
I drink 'til I'm sick, I smoke 'til I puke
Jerking off can't ease my mind

As I go to the beach I am reminded of how my generation of males worships the vagina
The tattoos they get, the sports they play, the tricks they pull on their bikes and boards
All in the service of their supreme master and commander the vertical smile
No, you won't see them make a bad move, why, not because they love and fear the living God

Because the social ramifications are far too great to risk being possibly rejected by the vagina collective
The males of America tow the line and obey the gash, nothing else takes precedence, absolute power
The slaves of the vagina have contentious spirits
They are driven and motivated by the possibility of gash and the superficial objects know it

How agonizing to live in a world full of vacuous souls like this
How annoying to see these pussy slaves raised up in our society
Truth matters not, God is absent from their thinking, all that matters is being considered
And oh how I cry for America, a sad tale of decline is hers

And finally my mind had been laid to waste by one last wrangle
Fuck Bill Maher
Godless, angry little pontificator that he is
Stumping for Satan, openly denying God on national TV

But oh some chicks have abortions because they have a little "E.T" growing inside them
"And the Christians think that Jesus will make it better."
Ignorant, oblivious slave that you are, you haven't obviously read the bible
Jesus addressed this exact situation clearly in the bible, learn the facts before you speak

Douche bag that Bill Maher is he doesn't realize that Jesus healed a blind man who was blind from birth
His disciples asked him if he was blind because of his sins or his parents
Jesus said neither, it was to glorify the living God when he was healed through Jesus
But Bill Maher still can't past the mention of a talking snake

God forsaken atheists in this country are gaining ground in the collective cesspool we call society
And that is why we are on the verge of collapsing just like Rome
Bad Religion is my Virgil, they led me out of hell, so I digress
But Bill Maher, Jesus still loves you

Good Night Sick world, I hope I can help make you better

Believe in thine cause, believe in thine heart
Walk with ginger footsteps, when the times are tough
Ride the earth when there's nothing goin' for you
We forget who we are when we're trampled underfoot and allow ourselves to regress into ugly mires of Doubt that enact negative actions and spawn chaos and despair.
Despair was the first real word I learned. Greed was the second, but then again,
Why am I always to blame? It seems that in truth I am guilty of every sin there is. A bad seed from early On, rotting with no recourse. Already rooted in the poison swamp by the time I began to bud.
Digging a perfect climb to attempt, someday soon.
Eminent death.
Could there be no other way? Small are my traits and disposed of for good.
What of my healthy corpse, how low must I/You go in order for the universe to set me free.
It is not my choice any more, it is my destiny.
Poisoned soul and battered mind, I lay to waste my thoughts.
There is nothing more to explore here, I need not go further down this
SPIRAL!!!!!
But the change will only come about through will, and that will must be divine,
For I have joined the lovers who learn to ride their tide,
Decide!!!
I decide to take it home, like a roller coaster ride you've become sick from.
There's no turning back just keep your hands and arms inside the car until the ride comes to a complete STOP!
Then, begin my climb back home and never look back!
I don't think I like the drops anymore
Believe me I've regressed, that was my third word.
I wish I never conceived of the concept!
I'm actually hoping to regress far enough so that humanity has it on its conscience how plagued I am.
The burden has fallen on me to pick up the rear!
The stone that the builder refused, will always be the head corner stone.
I crawl away now into another bleak night
Will any gift afford this?

BENEVOLENT ME, this beauty that I am
Whose dreams are able to endure the onslaught
Waged by doubt and demon want
Still a glow emerges from my crown
Still a glimmer in my eyes
Leads me to a new truth, a wisdom
A new telling that assures me that I will not be thwarted
Not now nor ever, for I am destined to realize my dreams
Should I cease to give up on them
I will see this through as I see things through
This chore is not impossible
This task not above my doing
This vocation shall not go unattended
I shall achieve what I have set out to do
In the fashion that I have seen fit to do so
I have fed the demon want 'til now
The face is emerging clearly
The self destruction is imminent
I will win the war within myself
As Michael won the war in Heaven
I shall persevere over my enemy
Glory will be mine
Surrender shall be my sword
And under it Satan shall fall again
I will be my own hero
I am Michael Engle
I am the arch angel

Bᴏʙ, I ᴅʀᴏᴡɴ ɪɴ ᴍʏ sᴏʀʀᴏᴡ, you stare at me from your "Rolling Stone" magazine cover throne.

And how your words have touched me so. You breathe life into my love, my hope and my plight.

You are the voice that speaks from your generation to mine, and to me you come like a victim of circumstance, destined to meet me face to face in my hour of grief and shame. I know you could not possibly identify with me, nor would you want to, believe me. I am the shame that America really wishes would just hurry up and die. I was born wrong Bob, not like you, you were merely "born too late" but that "simple twist of fate" has left me in the eternal shit house my friend. I'm ashamed to even address you as the case may be, but fortunately I'm ineffectual enough that no one will ever know that I wrote to you, including you, probably, unless your eternal soul reads this somehow. Maybe in a dream, maybe you'll see this in a dream. I've had some vivid dreams lately that make me wake up goin' "what the fuck." Bob, you see, I really don't matter to the world. I'm abandoned and abused, and I feel great pain, so, if you ever happen to read this Bob, understand that I love you, I really do, God bless you. Bob, you have brought joy to millions, in the most beautiful way, you have touched a heart that lives a generation away, and you have lifted my soul Bob, you have touched my soul Bob, thank you for that, thank you for being so omnipresent and mass distributed, for if it wasn't for that mass distribution, Bob, you may never have touched a reclusive deviant like me. Thank you from the bottom of my heart, thank you, for the words, the love, the music, the paradigm, thank you for laying the groundwork for a phenomenon like Rock and Roll, it touches so many and has spanned the decades to touch your humble confidant, God bless you, and God bless Rock and Roll. I'm merely a servant of the meek, a slave for the down trodden, but unto you I lift my heart, Bob, you give this human life a value, however obscure it may be.

Born into the "Cradle of Filth"
They shunned for my dirt
Made me feel like shit
Thrown away at the start

Help me to forgive
Like Jesus does above
Let me finally live
Not in anger but in love

Now that love has arrived
Like the inevitable dawn
In the shadows dangers hide
Sunlight turns demons into pawns

Opening now a book
Whose jacket is dust covered
The filth overtook
The book of love I have recovered

I will not try
To make you understand
Left alone to die
I felt their love firsthand

Now alone I redefine
And along comes and angel
And she makes me read the signs
And I find myself pawning her off on strangers

Burn me and stab me
Take away my grace if you must
Please Jesus forgive me for my lust

For as I fall again and again
I do it in faith of change
That there soon will come new face

Jesus trade me in for something new
Pay a little extra and get something worth having
I'm strong and lost, and of no worth

I bring you hurt, I bring you shame
Time after time, again and again
What am I going to do with myself.

Let me live, learn to forgive
Time for me, A time there will be
Wait and see, a time there will be

Oh Please Jesus Let it be

Can you taste the hate around here
Can you sense the fear
People so insecure
That they cringe as you draw near

God's will be done
I surrender again and again
And though I stare straight into the setting sun
I feel no peace at the days end

Just tired and strangled
Abused by the circumstances of every day
Bruised and mangled
By those who cling tenaciously to their ways

No platform am I given with which to share my gifts
No opportunity to speak my mind
And I despair that time will never close these rifts
Because of this country that is so unkind

They have set it up to be so
Dog eating dog until nothing good can emerge
And my voice each night no one else knows
And the unclean system seems to never be purged

And I strive this night to rise above it
And not give into to the anger and hate
This is God's creation and I will love it
And pray I find the Kingdom before it has gotten too late....

COMPLACENCY is everywhere
Apathetic responses to crisis after crisis
Purgatory

Competition is an infernal wind
Satan makes them think
Contention

I'm not playing
I still look like a loser
Obscure

What is real and what is right
Will haunt you or bring you joy
Humanity

The Sower sowed seeds, and his enemy late weeds
And when the weeds are burned and the wheat is harvested
Heaven

As the years go by, I find it more and more difficult
To imagine how I might make an impact
Ambition

When I started working in Santa Barbara
I never dreamed I'd be able to by weed at the corner store
Breech

Feeding the hungers has got to finally come to an end
A new life has begun
Exodus

Cornell West says he never joined the Black Panthers because of his Christian faith
And entire parts of my soul leapt into that sentiment
Vengeance is mine sayeth the Lord, and I shall be avenged
But I don't dare try to do the work of the Carpenter, lest I cut my hand and fuck up the whole house

America never wanted me, they don't want me now and they never will
I'm not cool, I don' t play the game, and I believe in Jesus
And though I am reminded that we are only sojourning here on earth
I can't deny the insane amounts of pain I have endured and continue to endure

Our forefathers designed a great and hopeful experiment in America
And today's American's are fucking it up so bad they may just bring about the end of the entire world
With their Godlessness and their contention and rivalry
I was born into a huge episode of "The Weakest Link."

Collectively America's values are as shallow as a puddle of my drunken piss
Not even that deep actually because I hold it like a camel when I'm drinking
Same contents though, just poisonous waste
And I just didn't possess the right combination of godlessness and good looks to make the grade

American's worship football and a big, hard cock
Artistically they prefer empty artifice to the quest for truth
American's collectively hate those who question the status quo, we all know
All I did was ask why do you guys put so much emphasis on sports
Why do you listen to music because of the image it produces
Why is it only OK to be fucked up the way you are all fucked up

Billions of dollars spent on porn each year confirms that I am not the only pervert
And everyone wants to come down on me for smoking weed because I'm not a rapper
But because I choose to question you America, I've been excommunicated from the Church of TV
I'm a termite and you are all the ORKIN Man

Don't get me wrong I don't chomp on wood
But if I did I would have been well received at UCSC
But as I expounded in the class about Dante, no one appreciated it at all
I was just silently awarded a diploma and ushered onto the first bus to invisibility

When I was younger I was crushed by the lack of acceptance
I writhed all night longing to be loved
Now that I have found my Christian queen you can eat a dick
But the situation hasn't changed a bit

When injustice is exacted on me publicly to this day, no one stands up for me
As a matter of fact since I have come of age, America has gotten much, much worse
More scared, more shallow, more godless, more competitive, and much, much more insecure
Be careful America not giving the glory to the living God

Babylon had riches and untold beauty, and walls that were thought to be impenetrable
But when Nebuchadnezzar's son busted out the sacred chalice to party with
God crashed the party and the Persians sacked that shit
I'll be avenged when you least expect it America, mark my words.

CRAWLING DOWN HERE WHERE the heat is hot, I find myself accepting the predicament,
I have to see things all the way through,otherwise, why bother to begin them?
Don't you see.
 I have to ride this until it stops, it has to let me stop, it has to tell me when to get off the bus,
To exit
The cyclical rollercoaster ride of adolescent misanthropy and social disillusion.
 My days of raping my esteem are close to end, I not gonna have a self to esteem if the ride
doesn't stop Eventually.
These mental bars are as thick as they've ever been, I'm sadistically proud to say.
I've gone and reinforced the stifling agents, these wraps of illusion that I wear just to see why
they even Exist in the first place.
Then I see they are the reason that man destroys himself,
These adopted surrogates, these mothers of sin that we nestle up to
And can never break free from no matter how we try.
I'm not behind the wheel, surely I wouldn't be so reckless with myself, truly any real me would
never lay Claim
To an act of self-violence, surely I couldn't be my own deadly terrorist, suicide bombing my
Consciousness and leveling whatever constructs had managed to manifest within
 My ruins of a skull. Where harsh winds blow a tiny flower brave enough
 To poke his head up amongst the ashes and devastation of self that truly remained, the abso-
lute horror
Of self atrocity, one after another until hope is buried by time and there becomes no road to
happiness, Only a slow road to despair.
We tread on, along this highway that is for those with no other road to travel, the eternal
dawn, always Taunting us ahead,
Urging us onward to a day when we too will live in the light of love the light of life,
A niche in humanity, a secure horizon.
We watch in despair from our highway windshields, the dawn
Of tomorrows that we just never feel, out of reach and somehow always happening and then
dissolving Just As we arrive.
The highway has an off-ramp but we want see the end mom.
We want to ride the ride the whole way, just for kicks,
Seriously. No it's really an ethical thing,
I have to keep my course until the ticket I bought is expired,
Until I reach my destination on the lowest floor of my trip. It can't be more than a couple more
floors now, Believe in me .Won't you, Could you,
Could I,
Am I supposed to or is it just that I forever

Suffer non-death?

The absolute derision, exemplary failure that befalls me.

The most perfect nothing known to man. I am completely stagnated in my own self

Perpetuating obstacle course of a mentality, torn between loss and gain, between engrossment and disaffection.

CROSSING OVER, leaving the port
My departure is near
Cry with me, heal with my hurt
Extinguish our fear

Crawling, lagged behind
The bitterest years
Stagnant, waiting to die
It never appears.

Sheltered, still under these
Immortal pinions
Waiting on a silent breeze
A scent of my kingdom

Alone in my eyes
Not in my third
I lie in the ice
And read a few words

Change is happening
I am not in charge
My pains are overlapping
An end and a start

Calm waters on high, so remote
I climb a few rungs
I'm old and dismissed, lumping throat
But something has begun

You don't realize it until you see it
With regards to the sheer gravity of things
A trillion words describe it to the utmost detail
But five seconds of beholding,
Immediate emotional response
Life changing magnitude
The Grand Canyon
A patient moments after heart surgery

And how life delivers the important things
And dishes us out our fates
Unhesitant and unequivocally
Like the big Texas Hold 'Em dealer in the sky
Showing you the river
That leads you into Eternity
And whether this life continues or dissipates
Or whether the river leads us to the other side

And oh that feeling when you are clearly all in
And you've been called
And yet the river card is still a' comin'
Only this game you can't fold
And how you've played this far dictates
Where the river card will send you
And who you are is your hand
And everyone is all in all the time

And to see the immortals surrendered and unconscious
 New York City, New Orleans, My Father
The youthful heart is stabbed
A Myth is dispelled
It all happened out of nowhere
So suddenly everything changes
And things will never be the same
You have to see it to believe it!!

Death will be a blessing, if it cleanses my regrets
Looking back is horrible at the pain that it begets
The haunted, tortured life only a dead man forgets

My heart was bleeding on the kitchen floor again
A lonely midnight snack remembers part time friends
A heavy reminder of wounds that have yet to mend

Alone in the dark and dying night I stumble forth
With memories of you like a bleak sardonic force
Another harsh reminder of what I am truly worth

All that's left for me is to improve my broken ways
Lament the times and places and all the wasted days
Though time brings forth another day, yesterday remains

A thousand sunny days stained black
A sack of pictures induces heart attack
Reminding me of what my life still lacks
Under this burden I will surely crack

I'M A SATELLITE ROTATING around a desert island
There just aren't many of my kind out there
Sub human rejects with problems like I have
Are absent and hiding behind blank stares

I'm a special breed of degenerate it seems
And so many will just never relate with me
They'll see my world in their worst dreams
But few could fathom my tragic reality

Alone like a hermit in the caves of never
I survive off the contaminated run-off within
So young when my innocence was severed
And now I must sever that which makes me sin

Detach myself from the flesh that has detained me
Starving the body in order to save my soul
I have wanted to change but yet I remained me
And these lost years have taken their toll

Jesus is sitting on the banks with his disciples
After he has risen from the dead
And I'm not one for Sunday school recitals
But his words keep echoing in my head

"Follow me" he told them over a barbecued fish
And I still can't muster the will to do so
Follow Him and with these sinful ways be finished
I have to believe that I will soon go

A transition must be made or I'll die in these caves
These dungeons of eternity that ensnare the wicked
It's not just a bumper sticker cliché; "Jesus Saves"
And somehow this broken abandoned heart keeps tickin'

I'D LIKE TO PROPOSE a diatribe
A denunciation of all that's taken place over the last twenty years
Literally nothing good has come of it
We just became more vulnerable to the end
More plastic, more hollow, and more egregious

We have a president that cannot be criticized
His ilk firmly believe that he is perfect
Any criticism is returned with fire
And yet he has made mistakes that stain like oil
More power, more deaths, and more stagnation

Music has collapsed into a hole of blandness
Films are regurgitations of things that previously worked
Art has become a business and thus become spiritually bankrupt
Television is so putrid that I can only take a dose at a time
More selling, more defining, more oblivion

I am scouring the reality of modern America like a scavenger
Eyeing the landscape like a vulture in search of cultural carrion
Revisiting things that had life years ago
Television shows, music and films that still have signs of life
More soul, more risk, more human

I listen to new Bad Religion albums that though still amazing
Are merely finely polished renditions of things they did decades ago
I have had to say farewell to my precious Pearl Jam
Whose sad assimilation has left them dry and unfeeling
More comfort, more marriages, more sleeping

My father's generation peers into this generation apathetically
Not fully comprehending the tragic predicament that has plagued us since five
I mean look at me, I have clothes and a full belly
But I'm barely alive being fed intravenously all that they think I need
More financial stability, more adherence, more artifice

Signs of life have become the target of persecution
Middle Ages here we come when the good looking people get their day
Neat clean freaks that discard all human aspects
Flesh covered robots whose soul has gone to sleep
More plastic surgery, more alienation, more heart break

And now I retreat from another day of isolation
Chilled to the bone each time I see another adopt that attitude
That fear is real and you are what others see
And as the "ivy grows over the door" I am sealed for good
More abandonment, more heart ache, more concession

Like a caged pig in a factory farm or a holed up veal calf
Made to live in its own vomit and feces unable to break free forever
Viewing the world from behind sad glazed over wearied eyes
My eyes cling to the remembrance of forever in order to escape
More freedom, more joy, more peace...

And more value than harvested meat for the insatiable demon bellies.

Domestic bliss is interrupted by sudden fears that dawn on me
Random ways I could self destruct
And as I cave in to temptation each and every day
Each wave resonates a little longer

I shake them off and get Satan behind me but as my sins persist do they
Like tremors disrupting a peaceful day
What if I make a lot of money could that turn me into what I loathe?
What if I'm broke my entire life

And how many more years will be squandered in sin
When will I be strong enough to live right?
What does it take to bring about once and for all
The change in my behavior that brings eternal peace?

Enter the thirtieth year
The third stage
The next level
The new age

I am so angry from the past
Struggling within and without
Struggling against the evil tide
Incapacitated by a debilitating self doubt

I glow but they hate it
And in fear they say mean things
They criticize me because I am a misfit
How I loathe human beings

Since I was very very young
I have rebelled against this wretched trend
And each day the loneliness stung
But I was determined to never bend

And turn into what they all became
Two-dimensional parasites informed by TV
Godless clones who end up all the same
Bland black- hearted bandits adrift on the midnight sea

I've been here thirty years
No end in sight
To the endless tears
To the constant fight

I grew up too slow yet too fast
Plagued by an appetite for deadly fare
And yet a self appointed outcast
Who still hasn't learned to care

For my rotting tormented self
Neglected and left behind

Always ready to risk my health
A product of the universal unkind

Another night I go to bed hungry
For peace of mind and cigarettes
And if I emerge to the morning lunging
I'll begin another day of regret

Put the past in a shredder and make the change
That's been needed for at least a decade
Stop feeding this urge that keeps me deranged
And put clean sheets in this bed that I've made

Thirty is now here
Reality check
My worst fear
Is to reconnect

Episodic depression and come downs that drive me to the brink where I like to call it a night
More pathetic confessions and miserable remembrance that keep my insides tight
Plenty of blackness that delineates the path of escape I've traversed again
And my dreams' obsession is tormenting me as usual, and I shiver with chill and fright

I wasn't destined for greatness this far obviously, I'm still bleeding like before
Only this time the blood is flowing over a dried rivulet that has hardened at my core
I used to at least have the hope in hell of tomorrow, at least something substantial ahead
But the horror that tugs me at my lungs assures me that I've a grueling task in store

Small ones live lives unseen, like ants traveling below the feet of the giants here
I carved a nice little niche here in the underworld, the domain of the ones at the rear
Crawling on numbly and humbly, we are a precession of rejects, unborn and yet blooming
Some in our precession have their terrible lives ahead, some have seen the coming of their fears

We dream with our souls for our bodies detain us, we call out to the spirits for mercy
We depend on eternity to explain away the loss and non-becoming that became our tragedy
We have no tears to cry for the ducts have run dry with our hopes and shattered dreams
And we lift our devastated heads to gaze upon our immense futures in a dark and distant
sea......

"...Found" it reads on the bumper of the blind
A Reaction to a more honest corporate sentiment
If your goin' to Heaven than I'll stay here behind
For I could never follow and resent it

Read your bibles translated by the scribe
Who's bled on your pages and ripped out his eyes
Read from the source of real meaning
And behold the error you'll soon come to realize

Albeit dirtier I may be
But then I'm further up the mountain
And any comparison cannot be real
For there's never any shortage from the fountain

A well spring of truth that satisfies the living
Is never a commodity horded by the competitors
The one who thinks of scarcity never truly thrives
Those who separate will owe eternal creditors

Fresh wounds today, new reminders
More reason to quiver and shake
Another reminder of my repulsive state
More of my happiness raked

She told me the truth,
And I refuse to take it with sugar
And the pain was so that I knew
I did it to myself because I'm not up to par

Another person left me today
Another heartbreak for me
Another time I realize
I am not for others see

I wouldn't wish myself upon anyone
My wretched condition will behoove anyone
Loneliness is all I can know, I am undone
My life it seems will never see the sun

I've got a brutal decision ahead
And a deluded mind with which to make it
Making plans for a future I may dread
If I don't change my life I will forever forsake it!

When nothing is ever going to come clean
The voraciousness of appetites becomes obscene
Slip away from dream to dream
Adrift on an ocean unseen.

Grief too strong for words
Arrests our consciousness
God bless us in the after-world
We who've been absconded

The climb has become a last ditch
For me and everyone on earth
We won't stop thinking of our own itch
And it's steadily getting worse

Get behind me Satan as you set your target on my joy
For I possess treasure you are dying to destroy
And despite my struggles and despite my wayward walk
I have been defeating you since I was a little boy

Like a thief in the night you threw thorns in my mind
That would strangle my fruit and leave me behind
But the power inside me is so strong it lived through it
And now I am an asset to the rest of mankind

And you thought being nothing would eat at me worse
And thought I'd give up from the sex and drug curse
But I feel alive every day and every night
And as sinful as I am, I still testify in church

Because I am a believer ever since I was a baby
I had dreams of eternity and visions of angelic ladies
Shooting stars and signs on the walls got me this far
Up out of Babylon, and just west of Hates

And so Satan will throw his condemning words my way
And try to make my past infiltrate this day
But every catastrophe he threatens me with
Is thwarted by Jesus to his eternal dismay

GLOWING IN THE MOONLIGHT lays my waning dreams
Starved by lust and addictive extremes
And through it all a hurtful hope stays
Awaiting the long awaited new days

Bubbling downstream like a babbling Christmas brook
Ice cold waters through a desert I forsook
Gleaming in the night like a dazzling jewel encrusted crown
Holding my stare so my weary eyes forget to look down

Like a cocoon that envelops a fully developed inmate
My condition leaves me clinging to my satiates
And even as I rot within my incubated womb
I still cling to adolescence alone at night in my room

But dreams fall from here like light sprinkles from the heavens
Within the mystical mountains at midnight 7-11's
An American dream that is destined to materialize
This will make such beautiful sense when the dream is at last realized

GOD TOOK OUT my two twin towers
And now I have nothing to sell
These two sites of my worldly power
Left a footprint where they fell

One stood like a Venus, dripping with sex
The other was a huge credit card company called addiction
And then two eagles slit their necks
And each crumbled back into perdition

Yet I stand here, not completely purged
Though not high in the sky for everyone to see
The ashes in my blood are toxically submerged
And these twins still maintain their hold on me

It's my job now to weed them out
And roust them from their mountain holes
Giving in to temptation, leads to self doubt
Osama is Satan, and now I am on parole

Their remnants alone are threatening the fabric
But back in the early nineties, they were running the show
How we used to trudge on so forlorn and manic
It had reached to the sky, what had started below

They need to be contained, for a while at least
Thus I must bring about my own personal Armageddon
And through trial and purgation, will be subdued the beast
Who only really grew as large as we ourselves had let him

And so there shall reign my thousand years of peace
Until it's time to do it all again for Jesus
This millennium sin and violence have increased
Cleanse yourself without delay, so the Paraclete can free us

GOD'S LOVE FOR ME endures the constant sins
Because truly he loves me despite them
Not that I am off the hook for heading home soon
I mean any day now

But God is there for each and every one of us when we need Him most
And I will eradicate my sins through love for him in his grace and mercy
It is love that moves us up the mountain
And I am gonna' look back with Him and laugh

When I pull into the station
In Glory

It's COMING time again
I gotta' make my way outta' here
And I'll miss you now and then
But I sure won't miss the fear

And if I left forever more
It certainly wouldn't be a crime
My life's chore
Can be put off for a hell of a long time

Bluntly put just too many blunts
It's time to depart
For a social gathering or a personal stunt
The puffing would start

And then Santa Barbara
And I can buy it on the corner
Good or bad karma
 It was easy to become a stoner

Again in this town
Wherever I dwell
King's Beach, Santa Cruz downtown
Weed hell

Turned a flower to a weed
I sat and watched God's majesty turn bland
That same old need to feed
Turned a golden oasis into burning sand

And how many more promises can I make to Him
Considering he showed me years ago
That unless I changed life was gonna' be slim
And yet out the millionth hit I blow

Please God let these be the final tokes
Let there finally be an end
And in those circumstances when the old me smokes
Remind me why I quit again

I don't need to be breath it
I don't need to be so distant
My love waits beneath it
My need for this plant

The money I've spent
Could feed many homeless a burger
It's why I still rent
It can turn me into a lurker

My lungs are black
And I've been too low pro
Just kickin' back
Or trying to not let anybody know

I've taken too much shit
Because I always know I'm guilty
And of course it dulls my wit
And makes me look somehow filthy

Because people can tell
And I'm too nervous and all over the place
It makes it hard to sell
When there's a glazed, confused look on my face

Because I don't want to have to keep going to the pot shops in SB
And drive up there every weekend
And wonder if they have any joints today for me
Because if I call ahead they get like offended

It's time to go to my path
And follow God's orders to the 'T'
Lest I suffer his wrath
Because I never chose to break free

Because a shooting star beckons me
Still lingering in my stoned memory
The magic, the transcendence, the glee
They deserve their rightful place in me

All I have and all I have known
It's all been defined by you
I've gotta' leave you all alone
Otherwise none of this has been true

"HEY YOU'RE A RIDDLE I say as I move aside
Like I really need your advice
You won't leave it alone,
Little men talk don't get a lot done

Livin' in sin don't move me either way
I got a feeling you're so vague
It's like taking a fall
Little men come when anything goes"
The Offspring

Little men indeed, taking advantage of an era where anything truly goes
Cormack McCarthy discussing rationalist crap in Santa Fe
With Godless data crunchers who still live in oblivion
Talking about how mankind is merely a bunch of doomed apes

These intellectual elites as they like to envision themselves
Will in the end be revealed to be total fools
Because they don't believe in God
Thus they don't see the whole picture

Trying to make these doomsday predictions from data
Collected by a bunch of dorks who didn't get enough pussy
And chick scientists who cling to ridiculous ideas about alternative dimensions
Arrogant in their blatant insecurity

All things that man has done will be made good by God
And all of these speculative guesses that these pea brains put forth
Will be laughed at by future generations
Who by the way will believe in the eternal living God much more than this generation

God who moves beyond reason will accomplish works that will freeze them in their tracks
Without the ability to articulate the phenomena with their rational tongues
Unless these sinners repent they will find themselves in Limbo with Virgil, or lower
And I am indignant that so many people give credence to these blind men

All of these things have already been foretold
And God sits in peace knowing this
Shaking his head at the arrogance of these lost ones
Trying to conjecture about the fate of the race

Jesus said to his disciples, when they inquired about the end
"Why do you look for the end when you don't know the beginning?
Know the beginning and you will know the end"
But this think tank in Santa Fe, New Mexico in 2008 is in the dark about the beginning

The godless ones will either be thrown into the fire
Or Jesus will knock them off their horse like Paul
And the Antichrist will be a charming rationalist
And many Rolling Stone readers will follow him down

"Tell all the people that you know, Follow me down."
Jim Morrison

How do I intertwine my influences this evening?
For surely they are interwoven in the eyes of the divine
Edward R Murrow with his indictment of TV and what it has become
Dante emerging from the pit to behold the glorious mountain of Purgatory
And an unauthorized documentary about Kurt Cobain and Nirvana

Searchers for truth, bold and controversial are each in their respective enterprise
Murrow spoke of how money and ratings made it impossible to perceive the truth on the News
Cobain talked about how the media pried incessantly into his private life
And Dante asked for the spirit goddess of poetry to stir him to inspiration to write the verses that compose the cantos of The Purgatorio

Murrow confronted a senator on a rampage of condemnation
Kurt confronted a music scene that had "run aground on the shoal in the sea of what we could be" to quote Greg Graffin
And Dante confronted a very real spiritual mountain with which every sinful soul shall climb

I can't get at the truth these days
The media is so skewed in the direction of ratings that truth is "absconded in the murky deep" thank you again Greg
And "illumination" as Ed called it, is seldom if ever found on the box we call TV
We are slaves to a capitalistic bi-product called superficiality and status
We prefer to be titillated by rumors of what Brittney Spears is doing with her puss these days
Rather than be edutained by things that will certainly affect each and every one of us
But these facts are "naked", as Murrow points out
And people don't want to hear sobering facts over dinner these days
They would rather be bombarded with existential nonsense and ego driven actresses
Walking on the red carpet of lies and parading around on the canvas of forgetfulness.
Instead of being captivated by real and pertinent occurrences in our world each day
American's choose to be distracted in despair by lust and decadence
Rather than hearing an insightful broadcast about affairs in the Middle East say
We want to watch the contrived drama of drivel like Survivor and the Apprentice
And because the facts have become more wretched than anyone wants to hear
Censorship is rampant and prophets are silenced and replaced by stories of clones like Angelina and Brad
Television has ceased to be a tool and become merely a transmitter of the plastic dream
A dream composed of constant dedication to image and perceived reality

Reality with a capital R has been completely neglected and Americans find themselves immersed Completely In a sterile bowl of antiseptic eradicating all that would potentially disrupt the reign of the Rulers of the Plastic dream.

These rulers consist of women with the anatomical makeup consistent with sexual tastes of popular media Of this day and age as well as dudes who have talents they have developed ambitiously in order to fit in to That self same plastic dream such as skateboarding, surfing and other professional sports.

Followed closely by cocksman and women who have the ability to attract a lot of lust driven perverts to buy the porno they star in.

GOD PLEASE DON'T let that cigarette ash start a fire
God please don't let me have obtained or transmitted any S.T.D.'s
Help me to love myself though I've been deformed since adolescence
Help me to get over all of the rejection I've suffered
Please help me to humble myself now that my pride is mangled
To be lost so young I can't help but hate someone
Poisoned and thrown away, drowned in my own self hate
Who am I to argue with your will?

You hold me through the terrible nights that I give in to
You heed my prayers when I am afraid
You bless me with the resources I need to live
I have a supportive family and a brilliant mind
The dog loves me and so do you
But I still feel forlorn as though I've missed out on something all along
I'm so angry and repressed
I've been so hurt

Let me remember the Roman soldier at the foot of the cross
He recognized that Jesus was the Son of Man too late
He had already left us, we had already killed him
True he returned again and remains forever but
I wonder if this pain will last forever
What could Jesus do for me, I'm deformed
I don't get blow jobs, I don't get laid enough
Girls don't give a fuck about me
What could he possibly do?

I believe, and I don't doubt that he will return on the stars
I believe he healed all those people, and fed thousands
With the fish that he made abundant
But he can't seem to help me
I am beyond help, I don't want to be helped
I hate myself and I don't want to live
I won't ever be sexy enough to make up for my past and she knew it
So did she, I loved them but they don't care
I'm just no good!

In bed I guess
Sex got ruined for me so now all I have is mind and soul
There is just no other option for me Dalai
I have to be spiritual, I have to pray and meditate
Others just do it because,
I have no choice
I have to do real internal work just to get through the rejected forgotten day
I have to search far and wide for the answers
I have to put this fire out!

I'M A P.O.W of sorts

I AM AN ECLIPSE, lost at sea with no trace of home,
I wander this dessert landscape, aware of my condition, squandering my little munitions,
I have no identity other than wrongness
I have no social place other than below
My familial space has been disregarded, and neglected, on both ends
I have attained a state of unaffectedness, a new learning
I have climbed the same hills as the greats; I have smelled the same air
They only won't have me, its custom now
The spirits are the only ones, the only ones that are willing to stay the course of my steps

I'm in Hell but incubated by the forces of nature, special conditions for me on this one
I was taken early enough that a perfect metamorphosis was catalyzed
My lust became a new agent of growth
And my hurt, my ensured destiny
Small are our sounds, us important ones
Don't be alarmed that I'm willing to go the whole nine yards
I simply see things through
I am the refuse that has some worth somewhere

I don't know what it is that always made me strut
It certainly wasn't the girls, no, it was the force
It was the movement of earth that created a nebulous roost
A stash for my soul, God hid me away where no one could fuck with me
But then again no one ever stays long enough to hate me
I shoo them off like endangered spectators
I retreat to my miserable loneliness in pursuit of the truth
The precious truth, what's it worth

Nothing in America- is sacred anymore
All the good things have lost their sparkle
Even the great hits are somehow flattened
Like the day old soda that got left open
I'm vibrant somehow! I'm alive as I've ever been!
Eclipsed yet cool with it for now, drown me again 'cause I'll enjoy it this time
Hope is gone for the conventionalists
There's only a new breed now

I AM AN incredible person
But not only am I an incredible person
I am an incredible person that has been dismissed by all of you my entire life
Thus my very being is rebellious
My very existence goes against the values of our sick society

I know I am not what you are supposed to be in this country
I am not ambitiously pursuing some TV ideal
I claim no attachment to a sports team(except the Lakers)
I don't have an image so I can't become a brand
Congratulations, you are widely distributed and bland

And now as record sales decline the parasites seek new nourishment
Sell your merch at shows, do commercials, sell out even more
Because the reason you are an artist in the first place is to avoid a real job
That's why the sentiments of your shallow soul sell so well
You on the same level as your sick adoring fans

So you win, I had to work a real job
I had to go to college and get a degree
Only to be tossed aside afterwards and left to fend for myself in a drying dessert
I had to actually humble myself and serve man
You served yourself and now you're lost

And I know how hard 9-5 can be
I know how expensive college is, and worthless
But I still can't bring myself to compromise my integrity
And try to produce a product to sell from my eternal soul
"God provides for the lion" and if they should know they will know

But as my daughter gets bigger and the costs rise
The temptation to become shallow and disgusting rises
And many have already become insects with no shame to their game
"The fox provides for himself through cunning"
And knows no joy in his day to day persistence

But a river of love runs through this vessel
And it is impervious to the society's attempts to keep me down
And the source of that river is God in Heaven
And there are no mysteries or enigmas to Him
And that which has been hidden shall be revealed
Mother Fuckers!!

I AM MONOTHEISTIC yet somehow masochistic
Misanthropic and sadistic
Born into the a falling empire
I alone shall contradict it

Men of ignorant pride
Rule my tragic arid time
George Bush and his father
Helped bring about this sorry demise

Men who cling to war
And soulless women they adore
Only savages assimilate
Blind to the devastation they have in store

America is a dream that has died
Its ruler's hearts and minds no longer coincide
And should you think me pessimistic
I would respond that you are merely blind

The day of reckoning is soon at hand
And with it comes the destruction of this land
I was born at the height of American glory
But I only witnessed the last hourglass sand

Jesus is coming for he died not in vain
And submitting these truths I admit brings me pain
But I'm monotheistic I trust in Jesus' will
And as America crumbles His truth shall remain

I AM SO ANGRY at sports.
The cheerleaders, the attitude, the aire of superiority
Over the ones who don't cut it
Like me

But there is good there
And I am to put aside my resentment
And keep a proper perspective about things
Through Jesus

I have to live this all down
All this shame
All this regret
All the hurt I've caused
The lives I have ruined

I bottomed out long ago and I am ascending
Still stumbling, sometimes committing an occasional atrocity
But not daily

I am trying to place the moment
When I first was led down to the pit
It was before the age of five
Maybe it was my imaginary friend Joey
Leading me out into the dawn light at three

The taste of sour milk in my bottle
The thirteen channels I watched from my bean bag
A seed was sown

A rift was opened that I was forever to fill
A desire
A lust
A Jones
A hunger
An insatiable thirst

My soul is indomitable
And I have fought against this for so long now
This war within, this war without
The default king

Doing what he feels like
Letting us all down
Refusing to try his best because not caring is his last line of defense
I surrender to the will of God

He has raised the ridiculous before

I AM SO OVER THESE rationalists thinking
Instead of knowing in their heart the truth
Proclaiming God is a figment of the imaginations of the weak
They lash out in their insecurity because reason alone leaves one scared
Our pathetic faculty of reason is not able to grasp reality
These fucking agnostic pigs thinking they have everything figured out
Are trying to read a book when they don't even know the entire alphabet
They simply don't see the whole picture and thus they conjecture
They compile observed data and think it is comprehensive
Yet they have failed to incorporate the incorporeal
They hate Christians not Christ
Which is understandable because Christians have been fucking shit up for two thousand years
But most of these butt fuck atheists hate Christianity
Not because they have contemplated Jesus himself
But because they refuse to accept that they have been wrong in writing him off
They just want to have casual sex and not feel bad
Or their ego can't allow them to change their rational minds
These kook scientists commenting on the future of mankind
In the dire pages of Rolling Stone magazine
A magazine that doesn't even have the sense to discuss it with Greg Graffin, the one atheist I respect
Blinded by the years of millionairedom
Being a millionaire turns people into dumb fucks almost invariably
It didn't for Peter Steele, Neil Young, or Ringo Starr
When I graduated from college in 2003 I was cast out in to a desert
We all were
A desert that lacked any real opportunities for happiness
And poverty struck me and hasn't let up yet
And people started groping for money in desperation
And as my reality turned into work hell, all the rock stars saw that
And they realized that they worship their money because of the freedom it allows them
Easier for a camel to move through the eye of a needle than a rich fuck get into Heaven
I am a profound leader of the human race but no one has the balls to follow me
People in America are desperate for social acceptance
And when people come together in groups in America they are worse than a bunch of Nazi pigs
One on one they are cool to me but in a group they always resort to condescending me
Lauding surfers and those with anatomy in keeping with today's standards
The Christians are terrified of me because I am not an ignorant sheep

The atheists hate me because I glow with faith

The girls hate me because I am awesome and yet don't follow their little pussy rules

The jocks hate me because I won't lower myself to their level and strive to compete

The business people hate me because I have a philosophical way about me

And many have sold their souls and worship mammon

And all alone I make my stand against all these Americans

I will change this mother fucker

I rebel day in and day out, and it won't be in vain

They have always wanted me to just die and get the fuck out of their way

But I will be heard, I will rise in this generation

With righteous indignation I will be vindicated for this atrocity

That took place day in and day out to me for thirty some odd years

People will seek out what I have to say

Even those who hate my guts because they won't be able to resist the truth in my words

And just as Chris Cornell says, "My place was beneath you but now I am above, and now I send you a message of love."

So will I rise from beneath all of you and show you the "meaning of success" as John Lennon puts it

Another shining example of a millionaire who managed to stay real by the way

My time is coming America

I am still an open canvas, merely because I have no value

Nobody has any demand for me, and thank God

What if I had become just another commodity, only I would be shabby

I ARRIVED AT A PLATFORM and perched myself above it
The pool of sin that lurks below
And I gaze upon the glory of God where upon the dove sits
And yet something still makes me go

I plunge headlong back into the red bloody pool
As if my skin yearns for the moisture
And as soon as I'm drenched I rebound like a fool
And swim back to the platform feeling impure

Only this time I am older and colder, and have wasted more time
And I am closer to the end of my time on earth
Again I'm forgiven as I as I scrub off the shameful slime
Only to ask myself what it was worth

My skin begins to itch and yearns for the water in the night
And a demon possesses me as I decide to head back in
Upon the platform I turn from the pool and face the light
The light that I neglect as I proceed with my sins

The platform is only the bottom rung of a ladder that stretches to God
And time is slipping away from me as I put off trying to find him
And as my body decays from the corrosive liquid I'm drying off
I realize I'm in danger of never escaping my dreadful sins

I AWAKE ANEW TO FRESH pain from a new nightmare
I scrutinize all of my deficiencies with my first waking thoughts
I chastise myself for being alone
I remind myself that others are not.
And before I can even get my wet dreams out of my satellite head
I need to give in to the need in order to neutralize the pain
Thus each day now, by the time I get out of bed, literally, I'm already heading south.
I just can't seem to get over this hurdle
She dumped me and I don't blame her
I've turned away from love because I can't face the day with her
So alone, so scarred and naked, so ashamed
Like an unholy limb, I wear my loneliness, protruding from my blackened heart
And now my damaged corpse has become unfit for the physical love I've yearned for and pined
away for All these years...all these tears... all these days thrown away
I guess I'm just living my life to the fullest!

I AWOKE THIS MORNING to find my belief
I looked to the clouds and found my relief
I can't go on worrying about how I'm perceived
I must trudge on alone until my love is retrieved

It seems to me that they have no interest
I'm reviled more than if I had advocated incest
In this rivalry we all live like insects
But Jesus doesn't say the same things as Jim does

I intimidate conformists, inadvertently dissing
I refuse to cooperate and off them I keep pissing
I don't fit nicely, so begins the dismissing
And I'm not invited 'cause their butts I'm not kissing

I admire the underworld kingdom of demons
And its will to persist though it's punished by reason
As I walk on alone through this lifetime of seasons
This constant pain makes me feel for those heathens

I BET THERE'S A whole sub-culture that's
Structured completely around being anti-me
A world that exists despite me
A place that does not know me intimately
In fact, I am quite foreign
I'm not like other guys
In speech or demeanor
I'm not a fag
I'm just super real and super serious about love
I just can't make myself go
I've been here for years
I know
But I don't go
I lag behind despite myself
I go into the wrong out of loneliness
I seek nourishment
I look for scraps among the dead
I seek out flesh in the night
My passion is too strong to be contained
God simply does not will it
But I will grab the reins
I will control my wild self
Because I have a duty
As a life form on earth
To conduct myself properly
So that I might lead an example for the next one's
The correct way
The truth of the universe
I was simply born wrong
And all my experience is in error
So I can help the most
To lead a crooked way straight
Is the purpose of Jesus Christ our Lord
I know, I get pissed at him too
My own private psalms
I scream my rage at Him daily
And whoever God is too
Is this all just a myth

Some story composed
For the purpose of justifying the lives of
The one's who suffer from cradle to grave
No, it's even beyond that!
I believe because I see how other things feel wrong
I've always felt you Jesus
And you're stoked on that
I listen to the soul of the universe
As Paulo Coelho puts it
My intuition
My soul
And it tells me come on already
And I really am pissed about that

I came into this world and adopted a mess
Forced to deal with paradox after paradox
Capitalism run-amuck
Culture sinking into entropy
And sewage in my brain and soul

And I can pass the buck on to those at fault
And sear with rage fueled by all I behold
But that is not what I was taught
That's not the way of Christ
But exasperation lends itself to hate

The list of things by which I am perplexed
Is so agonizingly long that I tend toward despondency
Simple tasks cannot be performed
My consciousness cannot elude
Being assailed by stimuli that racks my mind

What a sordid unhappy condition the world is in
Atrocities and insufficiencies are suffocating and ubiquitous
My brain is overwhelmed
My soul clings to eternity for solace
This broken world weighs heavy on my raw heart

And this horrible loneliness sets in for good
As I observe those I inhabit this place with
Hardly human anymore are they
Just drones racing each other
To the next illusory prize presented by a media god

And because I loathe it I am left alone
Cast away and condescended for my futile rebellion
I am too tainted by sin to sway them
Too devastated to convince them
That they are being led into darkness

But the one true God has foreseen all this
And resilient is my body, heart and soul
Resilient as the Earth's
Unfathomable fecundity
Beyond my wits is the solution

Thus I do my best to perfect what I have
And try to succeed not knowing why this task was given to me
A drop in a sea of humanity
A common man is me
All that I am, a whisper among the screams

I CAN BE A POWERFUL healer, if I begin with me
If I can restore my own vision by learning to see
Looking at the wrong things has furthered this disease
And it's time now that I go free

I've been shown what detains me, my tragic bars
The light is still eclipsed though I gaze at shooting stars
She's always very close, yet still so very far
And it's time now that I go free

When she whispered on the wind that she was blind and suffocating
Trapped inside my heart while I lie still debating
I decided to dig deeper and now I'm procrastinating
And it's time now that I go free

She will have to be the foundation of my new discipline
She will have to tug my stubborn mind away from sin
She's known all along, while I've wandered lost within
And now I'm praying she can save me

I suckle on forgiveness, like a screaming newborn babe
She nurses me with this every time I turn away
And her mercy never fades, though I rape her every day
And it's well past time that I go free

I've been rendered helpless by this random paradox
I hold the only key but I still haven't turned the lock
And all the time I've wasted still keeps me in this box
Is it time for me to go free?

Familiar demon urges well up inside of me
My yearning for satiation is a vast and vacant sea
Now the desert in me reveals my old belief
And it's time that I go free

It's time for me to wait down at the shore
It's time that I invoke the clouds to finally let me soar
I must prepare my soul, for life evermore
Because it's time now I go free!

I CAN FEEL THE PAST becoming non-existent
And like "The Swamp Thing"
I am rising from the murky deep within
And ever climbing

Closer to perfection, closer to God
And there are those who will frown
At what I have had to wash off
But these shall never bring me down

And I shall not be apologetic
For how deep I began my ascent
All larvas are pathetic
And each embryo is dependent

Nor shall I worry or live in fear
That an Ancient curse
Is drawing ever near
When I learn to rule the universe

Those who attain truth
And become light from a wretched state
Are beacons to the youth
And to the lowly, they can relate

But yet witnesses of great heights
They testify to patience
Inspiration this one ignites
And manifests the latent

I'M LESS CALIBER. I CAN LOVE MYSELF, I can love who I'm with, and I can "serve the servants"
But I will never forget that she is truly too good for me, I just don't get it.!
I always feel like a second rate human being and I don't really know why?

I CHOSE WHAT I chose and I hate it
I suffer and I suffer every day constantly and I deserve it
Who cares, pity party is me.

O.K, so how do I not feel sorry for myself
Just deal with it!! Like a man!

I just can't seem to get the hang of surfing, guitar
Or relationships. I don't know how to love.
I suck at everything because I've sat around smokin' weed for the last ten years.

Don't ask me why I became a sexual atrocity.
Ask Jesus, I don't have the clarity to answer that one this time
I don't have the patience to find a new resolution

Mother Mary and Jesus sit there still and serene as I
Come crawling to them each day desperately out of my head.
All I want is to feel good about myself

That's a dream, and like all dreams, if you don't follow them
They get out of reach, well guess what, it's out of reach
I just spent the day killing and loathing myself

The dream is fading fast, my life is becoming unmanageable
There is no getting out of this place, and that is just.
There is no getting over this, and I will suffer

They tell me so happily how I need to be alone
Well, for your information I've been alone my whole life
Easy for you to say you need time alone when you know someone will eventually come along

How do I accept that I've had to go through this with my entire childhood
How do I accept the fact that others have had good lives
How do I accept the fact that I've been fortunate and still I can't bear it

Someday I'll overcome this thing, someday I'll be free
What of all the hell I've felt, what was it all for
Help me Jesus to understand your will, I am nothing

I cut the three W's out of my life
Weed, Women and Whacking off
They were leading to the W of Worry
Will is a W I can understand
Work is a W that was a long lost friend
Why is a W at the end we understand
But it isn't nearly as perplexing as the dreaded When
Want is a W that leads to self destruction
But water has the properties that erode it to the core
We as a concept is our teachers grave instruction
Waste is life 'til now, alone on this desert shore
And wake has double meaning both the beginning and the end
It's a coming to life, a track of our travels, and a farewell to friends
Double U double meaning, both ominous and light
War it begins, and Wish as well, I dream of both tonight

I DON'T THINK GOD IS REALLY that pissed with me, it's the humans.
But I'm a product of their own waste, thus their judgment bears no weight
I think God is tolerant of my endeavors in his omnipotence
For he knows I had to go this far down to establish a firm doctrine
A foundation for a new faith, constructed of rational restraint
Yet founded on a philosophy of behavior which entails a bringing forth
Of all that resides in you, surpassing rationality is advised if not mandatory
There will be no martyrs in the new church for each will stand as an objective witness to the
Outer margins of rational being having explored the depths as well as the essential heights
(Of course making reference here to the idea of Beatrice, the divine goddess of love that tran-
scends all Reason in order to invoke the miracle that is love, and heaven)
Of that deviated realm that exists in the soul
And among the molecules of those quasi-intangibles we refer to lovingly as heaven and hell.
The Taoist would simply call one in "HELL" a person living in contradiction of Tao by way of
resisting
The impending, the unavoidable, the inevitable. The gospel of my Church is surrender, the
rules that Christ Laid down apply, Attendance is mandatory everyday but then church is where
you are.
To drink because it is in you and you're choosing to give in is rewarded behavior, sanctioned by
the Presiding angel, myself. To die in drug addiction is only to follow yourself home, it is where
the lord Wished you to go, and your life is glorious. To fornicate is fine, but fornicators may
not declare true love Among the community of church goers until said fornicators have demonstrated a substantial habit change (Again sanctioned by the presiding angel, yours truly)
Oh yeah, and one more thing, Christ is the King.

I DON'T LIKE TO HURT PEOPLE, I realized that at a young age
I live in a culture that gets off on it, sardonic subtle hurt
Manifest in womens' gaze, commercial apathy, and
Just a general lack of helpfulness of our fellow humans

I GIVE MYSELF to the river
And surrender like Mohamed
And pray to God that I shall be delivered
From this stagnancy within which I am bogged

Swirling like a cesspool
Immersed in the fungus and algae
I embrace the subtle current
That trickles through these days

I know God processes all stagnation
And invisible progress eternally remains
And so it shall be with my life and this nation
This pestilent bog will be cleansed again

I GOT MARRIED way too soon
Before I had my priorities straight,
I got married to the moon
And loneliness became my fate

Foundation and ideal she is
And I met her way too soon
In my youth of cold steel she hid
Until clearly I understood

Many talk of love but do you know
The pain of truth and the terrible woe
Do you know the woe it is to know
The truth and love and still not go?

Priorities, priorities a simple jumbling
Wrong things first and always stumbling
This golden key I keep on fumbling
I fell out and down the hill I'm tumbling

Sex is number one on the list, the best thing
Drugs are just a nose behind, the next best shwing
Love and health are behind these, and so I sting
These are my wrongful loves, my broken wings

But like a root she remains so I can never stray too far
Inside of me she always breathes, my private shooting star
I have been moved by a force inside my enduring heart
To tie the binds and close this rift that's always kept us apart

I GOT THE BENDS just like Radiohead said
I rose up from the depths to her height too quickly and got the bends.
I am lower than that now

I HATE TO COMPLAIN considering how thankful I am
For all that I have and have had
But it seems to me I've lived my life as a slave with a nice view
No exceptional accomplishments other than jumping through

Hoops I was forced through by societal pressure
Told I was not good enough and therefore must be
Relegated to the status of a slave
They can't wait to hurry up and dig my grave

Was I wrong to lack ambition completely?
To be content to do nothing with my time
Merely feel for life and seek it within
Perhaps having too little ambition can also be a sin

My heart breaks for my youth
Misspent, shamed and unproductive
My sole merit is my rebellious spirit
And that's just gotten me a lifetime of poverty

With no wherewithal, I kick around
Same streets and forests, I hardly ever leave town
I'm always too broke, or can't get time
Away from work, at which I am always the lowly slave

I have sustained significant verbal and emotional abuse
I always seem to think it's Ok for me to be treated like shit
I don't deserve better than hand to mouth wages
In my life I have never had anything more than just enough to get by

Oh sure my folks aren't bad off, and I can hit 'em up in a crunch
But without significant ability to generate revenue
I am encapsulated in this humble shell
And oh how my pride aches tonight

I know I was sick and annoying
And constantly letting them down

I'm just torn
Should I try or not

I'm downright discouraged
This dream keeps slipping away
Can I climb out of this hole?
And what will I think about, when I get old

I HAVE TO BE THANKFUL, though I fight against the truth
I still don't obey the law, despite the tragic lessons of my youth
And I just won't come out of this mental pollution
I just can't seem to muster the strength to create the solution

Please God give the time to perfect my gift and make you proud
I would hate to finally let you down and make promises of a tomorrow that isn't allowed
And I have to say I am obstinate like the Pharaoh despite my hearts professions
For I have persisted in my sins like a stark raving obsession

I lie and make excuses, I refute what I have told myself a million times before
And when the people closest to me urge me to come away with them I ignore
Their loving reminders because I am convinced by the enemy to justify
Another day living a half assed life in which I am merely getting by

I owe it to my supporters, for they have never left me
Despite my infuriating condition of dependency and poverty
But the lord has proven to be merciful so far, and I know he will continue
To guide me home to himself, and pave the way for all of you

I HAVE TO GET through this
No matter what it takes
Identifying the problem to death
I don't think I want to be awake

Altering my consciousness constantly
I pass in and out of pain
Things that I haven't done
Undone still remain

Collapsing into this each day
Unable to go to the light
Wishing my days away
Dying to avoid my plight

I'm pissed off, hateful and angry
And utterly alone
Drugged up and numb
Defiled and stoned

I think I'm O.K with it
All that's been lost
Because I'm eternal,
I'll survive my own holocaust

I HAVE TO RECREATE a new me
And rise from the ashes like the Phoenix
The enemy stole my youth
And I wouldn't have it any other way

I LAY BACK AND TAKE it all in. The poison and the gold
Combine in my body, and I am *The Alchemist*.
And I am the little boy, who still pursues his dream
Despite the obstacles and losses countless

Turning in me is the sap of toxic profusion
A battle I lost each day, testing the limits of my heart
I am sick and deformed in lustful confusion
And my pain is just about to start

I wrangled with the loneliness for long enough
And tonight I'm singing and dancing alone
I pursued my goals though the times were always rough
And I have come a long way with my heart of stone

I'll write tonight because I'm high
For the last time again tonight
And watch hope and despair vie
For my flickering life light

Surely I am loved by God
Just look at my precious blessings
Yet the past cannot be forgotten
As long as I keep forgetting

I'm over thinking it once again
A mindfuck lasting many years
Somehow finally I have to restrain
So I can banish all my fears

For many moons I've lingered now
On this ledge of Purgatory
But I'm still excited inside somehow
For my reward for knowing

But a cloud sometimes appears
So long as I keep caving in
I need a drastic shift of gears
God save me from this sticky sin

I NEED TO GET MY SHIT together, and then help my culture
I definitely see the error in your ways
As I stay here, making no progress up the mountain
Still taking two steps forward and three steps back

My sickness rears its ugly head, and threatens everything I have
And my righteous indignation is buried beneath the smoke
And so I am assailed on two fronts
But now there is beauty in my life

And to her I owe my best
The best me that I can be
And after I have made the changes I need to make within myself
I can teach my precious daughter how to not be like you

TV competitors, worshiping celebrity
Enticed by the two dimensional ideal
Chasing a lie blindly, and looking down on others in order to feel OK
Lost ones full of hate

Britney Spears is your Jesus, and you covet all that she is
And Brad Pitt is your master, and you hasten to develop his traits
Athletes do exactly as their told
And so very, very few think for themselves anymore

The corporate greed preys on its victims
Hording their profits as instructed by their master Mammon
Slaves are daily punished as masters with Lexus' blame them
For the slumping economy as we descend into chaos

And those who have revel, and those without covet
And the world continues to be devoured by the parasites of the human race
But the light of hope still burns within
For as I rise, the world shall rise with me

I REALIZED THAT I ONLY want to be loved by God
It struck me suddenly
I just want Jesus to be stoked on who I am
This is simply all I want

My hungers get in the way
My bad habits and sins
But no one is perfect
So faith is where healing begins

I once was wretched and there's still a lot of filth
But yet today the angels smiled
I think I did something somewhere
That made God love me enough to overlook all of my shit

I mean he loves us all of course
But somehow I saved my ticket to Heaven
Despite losing every worldly thing
I go off into the sunset in the end

I SEEM TO BE BURIED and forgotten
All that I had hoped when I was young
Torn between being ambitious and nothing
I try to remember how I became so humble

An emotion creeps upon me like a storm cloud
I try not to envy those who have an empire
Broke and unnoticed by others
But this must be where God wants me

Dismissed by my homeland like unwanted refuse
Forced to contend with being disrespected and written off
Everything that I am everyone thinks they can be better
And yet all I know how to do is let it be

Give myself to the turning earth and the sands of time
Watch them fall through the hourglass and obscure my life
A faith still lives in my breast that keeps me moving forward
That my time to rise and shine still lay ahead

I acknowledge that I have let some days pass
Riding on a marry go round of sin that I rode for far too long
But at the same time look at the criteria for American success
Superficial selfish self aggrandizement solely to get money

And I know that envy is derived from greed
Yoda taught me that
And my sinful indulgences I still cling to
Make me yearn for more than I have

But a child comes on the horizon
Depending upon her father
And will I rise above my internal mess
And give her the life she deserves

And if this feeling arises in the future
I might find myself resenting my life

And watching my child have all I wished for
Could make me weep for my humble experience

Tomorrow I have to drag myself to this job
That I am about as cut out for as a dog
And somehow make it work
Not just for me but for my wife and child

I must still manage to cling to my principles
Not just out of pride but necessity
For despite my material poverty
I must remember, it's who you are not what you have

I SHOULD STAY OUT OF THE BATHROOM unless I'm doing something productive
Or at least assisting myself in some way
I must work on my intentions and make better use of my time
I'm making a change in my behavior today

My identity in two dimensions is so insufficient that I've been forced to live in four
And thus in my rebellious state, I have been ignored
I have not wanted to change to appease their shallow trends
Or to become acceptable to all my part time friends

But if I know in my heart it's right than I can make a change
Not for some girl or some job or because some people think I'm deranged
But because love is absent, my fear constantly remains
And I'm fighting off the nervous breakdown throughout every bleeding day

I WAS ALWAYS OUT HERE, somewhere lost in the stubborn lie.
There is a shortage of the sentimental it seems in my case.
What a goal is love for me, no challenge greater 'til I die
I'm helping many if I find her, If I don't it's a huge waste.

Nothing terrifies me more than falling in love with someone.
I'm so insecure, I just can't allow myself believe that they will stay.
So I wander the desert of hell feeding and yet never done,
Only growing ever more aware of my tardiness each day.

Truant in fact from the school of love
Protected like a fool from above
Untrusting in the wings of the dove
And forever trapped in not enough.

Forge on in vain it seems today, I slept through all the sun.
It never worked for me to be with them, I always hated me.
That makes the blame so painful, for I had always run
That makes my hate so disdainful, and I am never free.

Know that this predicament was always real, let there be no denying
Understand that I was sent to sleep each night silently crying
Know that I lie awake at night searching for the day I stopped trying
Be it known that through all of this I have been daily dying

Like a nation that gives in
To the unrest still within
Without a miracle, I can't win
And I'll forever be consumed in my sins.

I WASN'T REALLY WATCHED out for and so I parish in this
I know I can't blame but I need a reason
Something to pinpoint
Where it all went wrong
I can't just tell myself
I'm wrong, and I need to change
I've always been wrong, thus you need to change as well

It's all stale for me now, the dream is flat and dead
I can't win
Where do I find the will to salvage what's left of me
I turn to my Christ, the first and last resort
We all toil in between
He's too high and mean
Then he's all we have
We trade with the winds, and bargain for our souls

Change will be made by you or another
Freewill is a paradox
We think it good
We need it
Yet it plagues us
How do I restrain
Where do I draw my lines
How do I construct a morality for myself out of this wreckage

What's a day of good deeds if you look for its reward
You didn't dig deeper, so you approached peace
A fragile peace, that's shaken each day
I think about now
And my place in this world
Never wanted
Much despised
By the disgusting consensus reality

In a world that turns us into products, robots and lies
A TV shell
Good references in the social world
Good standing on TV
An image lightly stained
With the right kind of dinge
That they accept
That they endorse
Me and my sex crimes and addictions have always been thrown away.

I've elaborated on my grief and still found no resolve.
I've acknowledged the truth and still been left behind.
Weary from my own devastating flaws
Cancered by own irritating sprawls
I want to have a life to live, but I am so outdone,
Where could there be any solace in abandonment of hope
Where can reconciliation breathe, if you have stifled your own sacred gift.
I have no more promises to break, or make; Search we on
For brighter day and lighter fate, for peaceful ground and contentment
Can we cleanse a lifetime of regret with our saged souls
And can we live to learn and be at ease with how far we've had to come
Can we accept the hysteria and make it real
And can we live free, but without an ocean of tears!?
Small creature am I, slighted much by them in deed.
Crossed over and pushed aside, or clung to in despair
I have lived a life of sin. Without any consolation for my eroding yearn,
I carry on, the wind as my will, gently tiptoeing through the rivers of blood.

I FIND AMERICAN CULTURE to be so wrought with contention that no one would dare give anyone credit for who they are unless there was absolutely no threat to the status of the individual making the offering. We are a mean people who frown upon what others are and who they have struggled to become. Please Jesus help me to be like the sun that shines on the just and the unjust in the midst of this mean spirited civilization that I have been blessed to be born into. Help me to become an expert practitioner of the virtue of forgiveness, let me drink from her cup with each moment of the day, let me forgive those who have sinned against me and resist my opposing impulse

I'M NOT going anywhere
I'm dug in
To all the ghosts who would try to grab me
Creeping in the darkness trying to steal away a little happiness
But I'm not dying off

All thee arrows fly my way
From within
All right you found the perfect way to keep me broke
Keep me stoned all day and tell me to sell copiers
But the fire is burning strong

Keep me distracted
You agents of sin
With lustful thoughts and staring
But my love with my wife grows stronger
And all is quiet on that western front

Like America in World War II
I am assailed from two sides, by two incessant foes
And they make all of my silent rebellions meaningless
But through surrendering to the will of God I am made strong
That which is weak, grows stronger each day

And as I assess
This ridiculous reality
I realize there is more that I can do
To grow spiritually, and emotionally
And I am humble

The Lord can use us as he sees fit

I'M THE ONE THAT'S BEEN rejected and alienated my whole life
Alone and living in shame
An outcast on the outskirts
Made to feel as though I am not fit to participate
Left alone in self hate
Even those who would try to befriend me were diligently and dutifully turned away
And the pain was excruciating like a crucible within
And so I turned to frivolous opiates
I took an anesthetized romp through hell
And yet despite all of this running away
My trail was still filled with tears
And my footsteps weigh heavily in the sands of time
Carrying the shameful burden of my shattered youth
And now as the time to stop running away is upon me
It seems incumbent upon me to become like this great spiritual warrior

IN THIS DIGITAL age of fragmentation
I need to learn to stop trying to do exactly as I intend
Rather become visceral liquid
And react to what comes rather than
Become a control addict.

In this my sleepy little California suburb,
Upon it's thoughtful middle class consciousness
Lies a secret of the universe
And upon my wisdom walk I stumbled upon this

The men have applied a bonding agent
To the early cracks in the ass-fault that is humanity
Upon new cracks within the ancient
To prevent the schism that jeopardizes the Whole's integrity

'What is what and what makes you feel good...
All these things I think about, think about
I always come unglued'

The unlikely prophets of America
Suggest a rift that has been carved by desire
Like the one between me and her
It's time we began to tend to this eternal fire

It all came to its natural fruition
Just as I imagined it would,
Not really, I was terrified by it

I went to the physical manifestations of my sin
The places where my name is mud
They can't hate me for loving, not forever

So I'm blind, and out of control
And I'm tearing through the town like
A quiet abomination trying to make a point

What's the point, that's the question
What are we after, another fix
Another satiation that lives and breathes

I can't live without tenderness, and I don't want to learn
My love is dipped in lust, I can't help that
But the only cure is so grainy, and alone

I desire to be loved, but I just can't love myself
So I just ruined myself, and left
I turned to the lonely road, and surrendered to oblivion

No matter what they deny me, no matter how alone
Love can still be my master, and treat me accordingly
My grave is comfortable as hell tonight

Because I know that you are eternal and you are my guide
My state will be shabby but I'm in good hands
Forgive me and I'm gonna' get up and fail for you tomorrow

If I could be saved by killing myself I would
I just want to reign with the lovers
I am lost forever aren't I?

This dark and mystical sea is overwhelming me
I am drowning, let it be known I drown in you
I just wanted love but I just am not fit

My life means nothing without love and my behavior
Demonstrates this grim proposition
And I'm going full throttle in the other direction

I can't take it anymore, I'm trying to do myself in
Love is just not feasible, I am too tarnished
I don't see how this whole thing could work out

But then isn't that what makes love miraculous?
Somehow things will unfold and I'll survive it and thank God
And for the loneliness I'll just come up with a nice excuse

Please don't let me hate myself forever Lord for ruining my dreams
Please help me to forgive myself for leaving these dreams unlived in
I'm so confused and my lack of understanding is tearing me apart

It's surprising how disgusting America is
And her children just as ill
Anna Nichole Smith
Could afford to buy her pills

And princess Paris Hilton
Has no worries of that vain
But just like Anna Nichole
She'll succumb to inner pain

Brittney's freaking out as well
Which happens when meaning is obscured
We've all grown up in hell
And we're a generation that's somehow impure

But those one's aren't nearly as sick
As the impotent leaders
With catchy names like Bush and Dick
Who love that show "Cheaters."

Late night ambush
They catch you with your pants down
Chaney and Bush
Defy the laws, they are always allowed

And 4 billion in porn
And Global Warming
A two party system torn
The Gulf is storming

But they didn't have insurance
And so nothing can be done
And so mutual assurance
That more destruction is still to come

Humanitarianism in America is merely
Superficial selfish acts
Transparent attempts that are clearly
Feathers for hats

Pathological obsession with outward appearance
Ubiquitously enslaving the masses
Hiding and lying, contributing to incoherence
While another day of war passes

They've conditioned us to compete against one another
And so we chase a carrot dangled in our nose
But shackled in debt and beset against my brother
I'm forced to slay an enemy I never chose

And my own sick head
Blamed on me from the start
They want me dead
They want me off their chart

I have grown in against the grain
Choosing to let them play their games
I have won the battle for my brain
And I'll overcome this country just the same

I'm not moving away
And letting the pigs have their way
I'm determined to stay
And bring about a new day

All those who depend on the emblems
Mercedes or Beamer stamped on their identities
Striving to keep up with the Jones's
To mask their insecurities

Are perpetually on the run
From themselves and no one
Always under the gun
And never feeling the sun

Fake boobs won't save you
A tummy tuck won't make you exempt
Anna Nichole was oh so blue
But Americans will still attempt

To buy their peace escape by escape
Into the world of sex and drugs
The consciousness forever shaped
By omnipresent ego tugs

America is sick, American history is sick
But I've seen healing take place before
If we could unlearn this crass and greedy logic
We could have a future worth fighting for

It looks like the only decision I can make
Is to grin and bear the pain like a saint
And leave these demons in my wake
Surrendering to God's will without complaint

He has demonstrated his goodness to us
But we run from the law and disintegrate our trust
We bury ourselves and then make a fuss
But we resist all existence and decay back to dust

Biting and scratching away at my self
I've forgotten my will to see more living hell
Only in theory do I know good health
I've been lonely all life but everything's swell

It seems inevitable now
Regardless of my undying rebellion
And the great people continue to die
Taking with them all the wisdom and sensibilities that this generation lacks
That Satan will get his way
The world will go the way of the Godless ones
The world will go the way of the superficialites
The world will be handed over to the competitors

Dr Phil shows up on every show in America
To talk about how he's intervening for a mess named Brittney
A victim of self, getting what she deserves
A mental breakdown because she's so shallow
And every show in America is about her
A sick nation that is so obsessed with this idiom
A weak people, no wonder the world hates us

Roger Clemens tries desperately to clear his name
They want to see him fall
American's love to see the fall
American's love to condemn those who shine
An entire nation of Sadducees
Trying to trick you into being condemned
A nation of useless soulless lame-asses

And I am chilled to the bone how alone I am destined to become
Not lonely like no pussy lonely
I mean lonely like the last living soul on earth
It's already becoming abundantly clear
That I am surrounded by insects
Who have forsaken their humanity
And given themselves to the quest for insect food

Insect food in the form of Daddy's spoiled little girl
Insect food in the form of "The Girl's Next Door"
The values of the E channel
Celebrity worship, Mammon praising
Self hate, body manipulation

Athletics, stunts and surfing
Satan is turning them all into insects

Their eyes become black and lifeless
They seek their prize with Hitler's zeal
And the allure is too much for even those who once shined
They too succumb to the illusions put forth by the father of lies
He tricks them into thinking money is what you need
Being sexually acceptable the all important criteria
And they kill each other in bitter rivalry

And as more and more of them turn into insects
I feel like I'm in "28 Days Later"
Seeing little sluts with no chance at seeing the light
Throwing an insignificant dis my way outside a bar downtown
And the numbers are growing, and the living are thinning out
Thus I continue to stand in opposition
But it looks as though God wills the takeover.........

It seems Lord that I was corrupted at a young age
My development retarded by some wicked means
And though my heart breaks and my mind is enraged
I still struggle with love, and the pain still hasn't ceased

Not a day passes now in which I don't break down
So much time passes and I just can't get better
Happiness slips away and death draws in around
How many more days will I have to spend in this rainy weather

Why couldn't I just have been introduced to the pleasures of life properly
Why didn't anyone intervene as I festered year after year
It's obvious now that they have all forgotten me
The real me, the one they don't know and fear

Thrown away and unloved I was left to my sickness
Internalizing this condition of alienation I began to hate
The self that I was that wasn't what they wanted
And never being able to truly have a clean slate

Women all settle in with their lovers
All of them collapse into others
The rocks are set in place
And I have been passed over for good

They overlook me so much
And I have no refute
All the damage brought about by my condition
Who am I to dispute

Alone is all I can be on this earth
All the joys of life have been ruined for good
I can't remember any time of happiness
And as things are I truly wonder if I ever could

Let this be an epic poem though, a comedy indeed
Resolution and recovery, or discovery as the case may be

All things are possible through the Lord as I bleed
And it seems it will truly take a miracle to salvage me

Things are happening that will eliminate my sinful self
An exorcism is taking place each day, a pruning of sorts
It seems it's gonna' be a long lonely trip out of hell
But I will see this vessel to its designated port

Forgiveness has to take place before the wind can catch these sails
And that wind is a beautiful angel, who possesses all my love
She is my impetus, propelling me beyond reason onwards in time
I just can't die until I respond to the sender of the signs from above

It's ALL WELL AND GOOD to sympathize with the devil
But when it comes to self doubt
We still might find it hard to revel
When self destruction wears us out
And we're forced to wrestle with words like never

Striving for a new idea, a justification badly needed
For the damage has surely been done
Stifled, blind, defeated and receded
Dusk to dawn, never see the sun
And soon the storage of miracles must surely be depleted

Who do I truly feel for, Jesus or Satan, dichotomy
I owe Him my life but just can't live up
And the other, well, at least he knows me
Jesus knows me but isn't fucked
I'm left with flattery and my expensive revelry

But I see now that I'm an Epic poet, resolutions found
I go down and justify it
I live though I'm bound
I search for truth and find it
I'll meet death with my head up and my heart proud

Depleted, receded

It's clear to me that there is a Life force
That is invisible yet ubiquitous and permeating all things
And Jesus is the Master

It's DIFFICULT TO REMAIN objective and think the way God does
While at the same time being subjective with your face down in the mud
When will my flesh succumb to my mind,
When will my mind succumb to my heart
For now my heart is in bondage, encompassed by flesh and blood

My love has become a weather gage of sorts, of my internal landscape
Of changes in texture and changes in hue, as I stifle her each day
Alone every day of my life
Incapable of having a wife
Love is a challenge handed down to me that crushes me with its weight

Its official, I am universally considered second rate
And I will never make the grade
Thus I cannot afford to allow what others think
Effect how I feel about me

I'VE APPARENTLY FORGOTTEN why my future was worth living for
I've made a pact to let myself go and then bring it to a halt
But each time as time arrives for me to start my chore
I explain away another day, and take it with a grain of salt

The lord has seen this episode, unfold each time anew
A mystified tromp through beautiful sights increases my desire
To find the truth and save my love and be once again renewed
Only to watch it burn from bliss to black as I jump back in the fire

It takes much faith to stay the heat, in both the heart and mind
For the former becomes easily convinced while the latter lags behind...

I've been enraged with society
For thirty some odd years
I try to do what Jesus taught me
While holding back the flood of tears

I walk with my head held up high
And know that all is well
Whether I am tiptoeing past the angels
Or drinking with the hounds of hell

I could harbor such a grudge
As has never been unleashed before
But I have been taught not to judge
So I'll exhale and hate no more

I was sick, angry and selfish
And you all made me feel so alone
Because to most of you winning is all
Integrity evaporates revealing a clone

Some will sit back and take
And give no credit where it is due
And as a Christian we must awake
From the conditioning we've become used to

But my boss does not strike fear in me
As he had hoped that he would
He didn't when I was a lost and lonely teen
And up to him I stood

The godless ones believe they rule your life
By assuming the role of some earthly master
But in the end I am always freed from this strife
As I will be in the hereafter

I'VE COME TO REALIZE it's as bad as I thought only worse
Slowly being tortured to death by desire for intercourse
Not just any human, that isn't going to shun me
I am surely being watched, by a raincloud and a sunbeam

Crawling to my knees from where I have diseased
Taking further steps downward in some ritualistic belief
Stabilizing only to scorch myself again, repeatedly
Perpetuating my own demise quite conveniently

I am not the fortunate one they claim me for
Fourteen years old. How could I know, the hell I had in store
Now years later I still bleed hard, from a fissure in my heart
In this crater from the start, at birth my soul was ripped apart

And now I sadly thus depart

Jesus can testify to the lack of unity on the streets,
People look at me as if I'm someone they compete
They wear their social merits as a badge that makes them proud
They're above and better and they declare it loud

They cast at me dispersions and glare at me with frowns
One glimpse of me in my dis-ease and I am then put down
Small again on the social scale, I find it hard to swallow
To judge myself on their shallow terms yet still refuse to follow

Overlooked and led astray, I've grown to become this
A reluctant piggy covered in shit, but dreaming of endless bliss
Eventually I'll start my climb, my ascension to my dreams
Yet in the light of social grace I have no self-esteem

My time has passed for "I'll show them" delusions
I'll look back on these dark years as a time of disillusion
But remember world, should you ever read this, I'm not the only one
You've all gone mad and hide it well, and you too shall come undone.

Jesus how do we not be vindictive
When we see clearly that we are abused
When the 911 commission confirms what was predicted
And egomaniacs make up another excuse

When stealing is rewarded at my own expense
And those who are guilty revel and sneer
And those who are victims seek in vain to find rest
And things came to fruition that they all along feared

Ego and greed are ubiquitous now
In this self absorbed society of modern America
And we witness an era that is steadily heading down
Lead blindly by a modern Judas Iscariot

Help us Jesus to endure all the wrongs
In the light of irreversible tragedy
Help us to rekindle those old freedom songs
And restore all mankind to its former majesty

JOHN LENNON was strong
John Lennon was right
John Lennon lives on
John Lennon was light

He persevered through the bull shit of human existence
The human condition, which apparently is that if you stand for peace, love and equality you must die
If you stand for something real you are a threat to the fake bitches who have the power
Richard Nixon was a liar and a coward
Just like George faggot-ass Bush
Clinging to power because he possessed no real power
Lennon was like Ghandi, Jesus, Martin Luther King, etc.
There are many more who no one ever knew their name
The world loves destruction and violence

John Lennon was lonely
John Lennon was brave
John Lennon never gave up the fight

So many are dealt circumstances that suck on earth
So many deal with it in head up your ass ways
Few find a way to rise to the challenge, and fight for what's right, to the death.
Not like some brainwashed dipshit following Bush into battle in Iraq
Thinking because you're killing in the name of something with stars and stripes on it
You must be justified, but no Vietnam and Iraq were as wrong as butt fucking your cousin

John Lennon stood for peace
John Lennon said "Time wounds all heels."
John Lennon was killed by a beast
John Lennon I can feel

I don't relate with so many of you, with your blind ambitions
Though I admit I am a bit too passive, I'd rather err in this direction
You may think I'm a kook but I don't want to hate
The enemies of peace are many, they are the takers, the rulers
They have small penises and penis envy, they compensate for their shortcomings
They lash out at those who possess the light, they try to dash it out for good

John Lennon still lives
John Lennon inspired us to change
John Lennon forgives
John Lennon was considered deranged

I just want to be in a good mood, that's really all I want
I just want to smile and love and be one, I just want to go off into the sunset
But there is a dark evil force that always feels so determined to put me in a bad mood
Because the ruler of the darkness can never be in a good mood
He does things to try to make the happiness dissipate, and when that happens war is right around the corner
Because let's face it, no one really wants to be in a bad mood, just some of us don't know how to not

John Lennon was dissed by his parents
John Lennon got shot walking down the street
John Lennon spoke against this government
John Lennon couldn't be beat

Killing Time
Numb yourself, drown all feeling
You move your body in vain
Consciousness is sustained
Pain is suggested but not fully acknowledged.

Thoughts of murder, others
Not myself anymore, they let me down too!
I can't blame my parents for what happened to me entirely
They tried their best for us in capitalism
A lot of the blame falls on America

The nebulous entity that is America
An idea that is so beautiful it becomes fascist
Yes fascist, America is a fascist county
The SS is MTV, the gas chambers are filled with the uncool
These rejects that America has abandoned
Are not totally interested in the X-Games or even just having fun
We don't have perfect anatomical structures according to the
90210 American world that
Sees only with its eyes

No we're taught to hate ourselves, those who are subjected to Americas gas chambers
And the death is slow. Slower than the original death because it has no name
And kills you slowly in bits and pieces

Dissed
So hard a hundred times a day
Since I was five frickin' years old
But Jesus says to love your enemies so I'm tryin' to love myself:
My coaches, my peers, the hot chicks, the cool chicks
The popular chicks, the beautiful chicks
The fat chicks, the jocks, the drug dealers
The cool dudes, the skaters, the surfers, the snowboarders
The studly lookin' dudes with big enough cocks
The commercials that tell me my cock is too small

The bartenders, especially chick ones
The priests, the GOOD people
The sheep (I mean the humans, I have nothing against the animal and don't want to fuck one)
Have taught me to think
It's all my fault
Oh I know you don't want to hear about it
That's why I got thrown away, no one wants to hear about it

Her troop of elites are just too sellable
I have no market value you see
I'm just supposed to accept things I guess, pretend it all away
I'm just supposed to let go of what you meant to me and carry on as though
I deserved it all along
As if I was born to be dissed

Lao Tsu believes that man "resorts to virtue"
Only after he has failed Tao
Yet Christ says "Whoever wishes to come after
Me must deny himself."

This contradiction leaves me stranded in a lonely desert outpost in ethereal eternity.

Life has slipped from me in some sinister way
As if I've been assailed by some magician of darkness
A being that has control of my head each day
A beast that has ruined my every season's harvest

Every time I start to get mad at her for leaving
I just stop and realize that I have been locked out
And I go on shocked and disbelieving
There's only room for one person on this escape route

Like a bitter real nightmare, so terrible is it
Haunting me with what could have been
Like a lid on me that traps me here within
My life defined by the cruel and obscene

I can't help but dwell on my problems
I don't see how anyone could help
Like Augustine I keep falling
Because I was born in Hell

Stained with this terrible goop, I moan and have fits
To be condemned to live forever in this pit
I stay alone without profit, my burden no benefit
How will I rise up out of my shit?

That question will be answered, if it be my destiny
For I've always refused to be a tragedy
When I stop wussen' out, I'll finally break free
And like an epic hero I shall rest happily

Love is a ladder upon which I am to climb
Blind and resentful I await the right time
And I'll let it go, all this time that's gone by
And I'll wear my swamp wounds until they dry

LIKE A PRISON is self hate
Like a virus that contaminates you through TV
There's nothing more dangerous to a subject
Than to be convinced that they are inferior
To come to the conclusion that they are merely
A deficient commodity!

Once you become aware of what they have deemed a deficiency
Internalization brings about a profound self destructive tendency
These tendencies are latent at first then become manifest
Usually in the form of a host of self defeating behaviors.
For me that was drug use. A quick escape from the constant pain of not cutting it
Also a constant satiate that pacifies, or at least the mind convinces itself,
That it's pacified, only to create a deeper well of desire within the
Programmed subjects viral consciousness

Sex, a constant drain on my consciousness
A desire for which is instilled at every corner
Of the assimilated subjects consciousness
The libido, in me born too soon, is constantly
Tugged at in our culture being that sexual potency has become a mandate for
Happily married men and women, or respectable people anyway
Unfortunate are those who have been deemed unattractive, or even worse sexually repulsive
For theirs is a fate tragic should they succumb to desire.

My whole life I have been made to feel like
I don't cut it, for the girls at school, or anyone for that matter,
Yet my libido, again born too soon, is constantly being stimulated by the TV
Ruled American culture of which I am an unfortunate subject,
I have committed many a sexual atrocity in mindless pursuit of satiation
At whatever cost to myself or others involved

Now though this may seem selfish I offer no apology
America got what they deserved in Me!

Like Augustine I put off
The journey to my Lord
And the swamp became a trough
In which more slop is poured

And I have lingered on this ledge
And God's great Love endured
Like Augustine my soul remains
With chains and locks secured

And Jesus came to me and rebuked me
And asked why I call him Lord
When I refuse to obey my King
Even after I hear his Word

But Satan knows and he is bummed
That I will emerge victorious
And the myriad times that I succumbed
Will be miraculously glorious

And as this world heats up like Hell
And the competitors take their turn in the sun
And as everyone scrambles for something to sell
My journey home has yet begun

And my angel on earth has merely started her shift
Keeping the light alive in the race
And God would not go and squander his gift
So I can be patient and just keep my pace

Like illness does, so goes this demon
Slowly but surely, infiltrating my dreams
Poisoning my prey, that which I ingest.

It is through the feeding that he moves
Each new pleasure devoured, decomposes
And wreaks havoc upon my love, it's prey!

Savvy and crafty, he ruins our love
And it takes time to restore, and sometimes nevermore
This is why our loves must be restrained.

If our lusts and pleasures become wicked endeavors
Only welcoming un-health, and corruption
We must let him starve to death, or smile as we let him in!

Like taming a wild beast
Or evolving into a new one
We can learn new traits
And reverse all that's been done

And start to save ourselves
And hopefully save others
If only into truth our eyes should delve
We could all live with one another

There is no such thing as scarcity
Only a mentality that consumes
I don't need to hate you, you don't need to kill me
There is always plenty of room

The past can be gone for good
Permanent alterations can be arranged
And the Word can penetrate every neighborhood
We can assimilate to that which seems strange

Whether you believe in God or not
These changes can be made
It is not my fate on earth to rot
That fate I can choose to evade

Nothing is irreversible
It has never gone too far
The fountain is eternal
We are born anew like the stars

And should we be taken up for good
At least let it be because it was time
Not because I never understood
And far too soon chose my own demise

Loneliness is the cause, my Lord
I cannot bear this arid prison cell any longer
Thus I fall, again and again
I still may overcome, I still may finally have my exodus
Just not today!!!!

Looking back on prison life as it is
I feel a strange acceptance tonight
Is it because I have drugs, is it because I'm free
Or is it because I believe again

I am destined to remember that even should I never marry
Even should I never have sex again
Should my flesh never rub against another's
Should I wither away in a cave like an exile confined
There is a force that will eternally comfort me
In my time of dying she will be there

I can take this on
She has never left me
She is watching and waiting, for me!

Love comes and visits the living, asking those of us
Who've always been going down to reconsider some time
The time that's been wasted, the beauty that's overlooked
The dreams easily forgotten that must be revisited

She beckons us to think on the wisdom that's managed to find its way in.
I have no form in writing or in voice
Nor in physical being.
My body merely a vessel that demonstrates the symptoms of my soul
Atrophied and despaired, I almost can't see it happening this time

I'm all words, I'm all advice and no show, I have no place
Among the living. There seems to be no way out.
Why does my heart continue to beat? Only God knows
There must be some beautiful cause for this much wreckage, truly

I am a warning sign to the dangers of neglect
I don't tend to myself, I have nothing left to tend to
Nights race by in anxious wonder, only to be finally revealed as another waste

Crying isn't possible for me, I've brought this on myself, like some kind of destiny
I roll on through the days towards my death and my release
Praying that the latter precedes the former

For now I rot in peace. Nothing closer to despair than untimely death.
Can wisdom redeem me, can she change the way I live
Can she free me from my own mental chains

My brain bears an enigmatic tendency to wreak havoc upon my very consciousness
There something poetically, metaphorically, beautiful about the secrets of self destruction
The way our self induced suffering finally does us in
Some of us don't go down as quickly as others

Some of us cling to belief in some kind of resolution
A miracle on the burning horizon
A time of escape from the social pollution
Into a person that someone relies on

Look close and you'll see that I have been infiltrated
A child born into a mire within
A messy existence can't be elevated
And I've lost my medal while living in sin

So long in limbo, it must be that I'm a sign
Pierce would find no joy in it
Nor would the moderates who act by design
Only large hearts survive the pit

The lovers dance in bliss in a higher realm
I am innately below in here
Looking at the wounds that will overwhelm
A weaker heart to fear

A COLD WIND BLOWS through my weathered soul
It is what replaces the warmth of love
Looking up can take its toll
Gazing at the blessed above

Some lives are tragic, lonely and unfortunate
This one seems to be so
A stubborn vile insubordinate
That's always been alone

Love your enemies!
As countless as they are for me
The tattooed competitors lingering on the corner
The crass, aggressive drivers speeding in the rain
The superficialites living in two dimensional worlds
Television, My Space and the movies

A Brittney world
Ruled by unconscious drones
Desperate to dis so they can feel good about themselves
Ambitiously seeking money fame and fortune
Without regard to integrity
A puddle deep revolution

Say hello to your neighbor
And when they don't say "Hi" back
Because they want to seem cooler than you
And they are trying to make it clear that you just don't do
Remember Jesus said to love them
Find room in your tattered heart

Rolling Stone magazine
Has become the final word in all that matters here
And they don't represent you well
Your favorite bands go unnoticed
They applaud Eddie Vedder for becoming a clone
Love and "Let it Be" like the Beatles

And John Lennon
Who merely said the same
Was researched by the FBI
Despised by his parents and peers growing up
Forced into seclusion by the insect media
And finally killed by a roaming lost soul

And a 13 yr old named Eric
With red hair and a philosophical tone
Tells "48 HRS" that he knows how he killed that little boy
They fucked with him at school, relentlessly
His step dad said he was a worthless piece of shit
And the rage inside spilled out

And the kooks at Buena High School
Who did the same to me
The parents, the teachers, the kids all the same
Scared to death of this new kid from LA who was cooler than all of them
Then they systematically tried to eliminate him completely
All but had me killed

And every check stand at the grocery store
Pushes my rage buttons each day
Weight loss messages every two inches
Scared, lost, desperate girls patting themselves on the back for their appearance
On the cover of the next dime store rag
She did everything they told her to

Put all the rage into a box and mail it to God
Give it all to the omnipotent King
Don't just silently sear inside
Truly let it go
God brings rain to the just and the unjust
Jesus said to love your enemies!

Many moons have I passed in this way
Many storms come at me
I am so buried in this crap that escape seems
Like a dream, a stale dream

I can't go on living without the sun
Creature of the night I was born
When will I start the battle for myself
When will I finally be liberated from these binds

My will is all but crushed, yet I go on
No one knows or cares about how I hurt
No one can relate with my sorrow
It's as if I don't really exist

Crawl on I will, drag my being onward
Towards a certain sun. A comic end
I am faithful, yet tested, tried and challenged
I can't be solely to blame for all of this

ME AND JIM HAVE one thing in common, the quest for eternal bliss
Eve may have thought we needed knowledge but I just throw it away
I'm down with Paradise
I like peace
"Now I'm on my own,
Castaway"

I'VE HATED MYSELF my whole life for the way I look
And that's all but destroyed me
In a TV culture where you're supposed to be hot and yummy
Our emphasis resides along the surface

My ribs collapse inward from the strain of this limitation
And every day I rage against it
A less than human being that no one wants
And my pride just won't accept this

Every day I wake up remembering why she left me
We are both informed by the same data infrastructure
A television consensus which has declared me unappealing
Apparently what I am just never suited the networks

So, on I trounce, in delicate despair
She was just out of my league
I'm in the miscellaneous
Anything goes
Racked with deficiency
Shabby
You get what's left league

A hierarchal structure of value in which mine is close to least
And yet somehow I'm supposed to love myself
I'm to accept that others are better and put them before me
And not many are interested in me

And the reason they are interested in me is no fun, they like to talk to me
I'm cool to hang out with and watch a movie, sometimes I'm funny
Why has God cursed me in this way, why couldn't I have been appealing?
I got dumped, thrown away, selected against

I'm supposed to be nice and deal with my station in life
I'm supposed to be mature and accept my lot in life
I'm supposed to somehow find a way to love myself
Even though she's getting fucked by someone else
It looks like I've been gettin' some too, Yeah, love what I get
I choose from who would have me, not who I want

Why am I so cursed?

My anger looms
And is sleeping inside an anesthetized mind
In secret rooms
Live out the lives of those left behind

I left Ventura
To escape the mentality of the competitors
And in Tahoe
I was privy to the wretched X Games pioneers

Then to Santa Cruz
For the X Games apex and the immoral majority
And now to corporate America
With the backstabbers and the materialistic authority

Another formidable challenge
Christianity seems all but impossible sometimes
How I manage
Is a mystery amidst the contention and sex crimes

Weed my sweet
You have assisted me in this painful coming forth
Emerging from the abyss
With a glowing ball of forgiveness for what it's worth

But now we must part ways
The Creator has revealed it to me and yet I persist
Clinging like a slave
To the only ticket out of pain when I am hurt and pissed

And now I rest
And pray to God to help me to let the anger go
And beg him to forgive me
So that finally another reality I might know

My bitter lonely life beats on
My sins are chased but not undone,
Cries from within my sick mind ring
Broken hearted forever, in the desert wandering.

Burned alive by my own two hands,
These feet now stumble on
Through dark towards death
In a daze from all that's wrong

I am cursed to witness,
My own nemesis,
Destroying me from within

I am cursed to wear
My own dumb stare
A victim of my sins.

My ego is so lashed
Like the back that has been scourged repeatedly
And the girls still wonder why
I'm sensitive when they say mean things

My physical attributes have always been a joke
My red hair, and the rest
Why did God give me the lion's share of short comings?
Why did he put me to this test?

I get no rest
It's everything I can do to keep fit
Just to get laughed at and mocked
And they wonder why I'm oversensitive

I'm just supposed to laugh it off
When I get no attention
And I go from being an ugly kid
To a gross senior citizen

No matter what I'll never be enough for me
Jesus is there to comfort the castaways
The meek
The weary
The stone that the builder refused

I have always been rejected by my TV mind
And I don't even try to keep from being left behind
I try to get some sleep without getting high every night
This world at once so beautiful and yet still so unkind

The glorious moon and stars, the majestic mountains and the seas
Impervious to the horrors that permeate my life of disease
And though it's all so perfect no one cares to hear my pleas
For retribution, justice and some miraculous reprieve

My generation declines
As the things that were good are blaring in our face
And as this predicament defines
Nothing good can be found anymore, anyplace

We cling to the past
Assuming roles that were illuminated before
And they stand aghast
Those of old who stand witness to what's in store

Democrats and Republicans
And musicians conforming to unbroken molds
Clones and replicates
And personalities that are doing what they've been told

And California inundated
With gruesome searchers clinging to the TV ideal
Privacy eradicated
By envious nothings desperate to stab and steal

Immature parents
Instilling a savage lifestyle in their tragic youths
A culture errant
Ravaging each new day devoid of truth

A tidal wave of sewage
Has washed over me and drowned me out
Clinging to a buoy
I strive to relinquish despair and doubt

If only some agency
An avenue of social reform and renouncement
To prune the pagan tree
Through widespread internal endowment

Rage inside me
Bubbles into an inferno each time I go in public
To gauge this dark sea
I must find my way home by escaping from it

My IDENTITY IS defined by a lack
And my consciousness is forever shrouded in darkness
You get to live and I don't
You get to receive and I don't
Always hurting always hungry
My entire life has been lived
Cast away into the shadows
Forgotten and abandoned
Left for dead
Supported by a force
From which I am divorced
Absolute dichotomy
And my consciousness is forever shrouded in darkness

My life is a bitter torture
Each second brings stabbing pain
Every moment a new hardship
Every moment another escape

Beautiful scenes inside my dreams
Torment me from within
Something missing, something gone
There's something wrong with my life

Christianity punishes me
What I want is not there
Some fading Paradise elsewhere
Haunts me and I am overcome

Some vacant beauty
Some rousing pain
Stirs me from my salvaged slumber
And reminds me that I lack

Some vision of youth, some idea of yesterday
I've crossed the line too many times
Hollow is the dream, the house that haunts me still
Long vacated by the life that breathed there

Now in my empty chasm I sit
A requiem for time that passed
I just couldn't grab it and make it mine
Thus it taunts me with its eerie wake

Some vision, some dream
Some idea that was my home
Estranged and lost from it
What darkness, what woe

Grave confusion, life passed me by
Nothing to show for where I've been and what I've experienced
All is lost, the dream plagues me
And now I only know loss

A CAVITY CAUSED by a mystical setting
That I squandered unaware
Leaving me with shattered dreams
And a lifetime of despair

MY LIFE IS COMPOSED OF a desperate longing, and overstimulation is my method of escape.
They would only call me sad and jeer me while my love is raped
Falling daily in search of worth, I reach out for a brand new birth
But each day I am teased with what I can't have, and I am left only to wonder what love really feels like.
Small and insignificant, I can handle that I guess. But forever truant and displaced I find too strong a test,
My strength gives up and I let myself go, for the millionth time in vain
 I think I might forever be left stricken with this pain

MY PEACE IS at times compromised
But my faith is unencumbered
I have sinned and I have been despised
But still my blessings cannot be numbered

True I have been deficient and yelled at God
But yet I roll within even through these times
Unhappy so much of my life, and mankind on the nod
But yet my spirit remains unbroken and sublime

And though some people get pissed at me
Mostly they are scared of the faith I walk with
And I am constantly under the gun unseen
And my faith remains unshaken even at the gates of Dis

Abraham, Joseph, and all the Israelites
Know the gift given to those who believe
Through slavery, oppression and the last rites
We possess something impervious to thieves

And how does the eternal story apply to us
Who are today's Hebrew slaves, where is Egypt now
I am Joseph and the Pharaoh, dipped in modern lust
And though the tension gets quite thick, I'm free somehow

And in anguish and despair I admit that I am tragically flawed
And through winds of doom within I have bowed and crawled
And I won't deny there are many of whom my actions have appalled
The life of a misfit in bedlam, my faithful soul gracefully endures it all

Now beckons me frighteningly into awareness
The lateness of the hour, the important time at hand
The evening grabbed me and sat me down
The important decisions of my life are upon me

Paralyzed by the overwhelming state of things on earth
Stalled within as I lost another day to sin
The night got cold and desolate, and the truth was bearing down on me
As I withered away as the world withered

My life passed before my eyes and how fleeting
So few things have been accomplished in these many days
Life has to begin soon, I need to emerge from the cocoon
This darkness inside overtakes the calm patient warrior

Anger in all ports of call, and immigrating here illegally at an alarming rate
Republicans and Democrats take their turns fucking things up worse
Vengeful hotties in BMW's, kooks in suits, egomaniac bosses
That mixed with half a joint of the chron is enough to stop the world

Race wars, earthquakes, and a whole lotta' talk of Armageddon
Sex talk, computer viruses, debt growing, China owns us
But fortunately the Lord works wonders beyond reason
And where one knocks the door will be opened, eventually

Thus the night has been regained, and the hope warms again inside
A revolution is at hand, a huge disgusting one, in which justice is done
The exodus home has begun, the prophets have heralded the time
Out of our personal Egypt, through our own Red Sea, to our own kingdom within

Now well past the corporate takeover
We regurgitate what we felt yesterday, because the present is an onslaught
An aftermath of the now, and a year left of Bush
And plastic surgeries are way up

Thirteen years since Cobain departed
And still those same old feelings, who the fuck am I really
An athlete that failed to try, someone who appreciates good music
But never was encouraged to play

Humble circumstances, no money and a loving home
And yet as alone as I was then, and burning with rebellion
What should I be ambitious about, I remain outside the race
Just moving slowly in self propulsion

I can't tell if it's the weed
Or if I have a Nietzchean reactionary morality devised out of opposition
To the ruling TV superficial majority, who compete with their skin
And yet slowly rot within, bringing everyone down along the way

And Tom Petty verbalized it well, watching with his own eyes
The sad demise of a beautiful thing, every ounce of soul sold
And a price tag placed on every phenomenon, and if the magic is real, the price goes up
And as incredible as his life has been, this thing has left him weary

All of us with embers lurking beneath the ashes of our lives
Are weary of the fight, as the streets becomes overrun with the Mammon worshipers
Making rock stars on the Gong Show, and starving themselves for attention
Because they are starved for attention, because they have vacant lives

I have no ambition, I can't bring myself to hustle
Pitted against my brothers and sisters, and forced to make cruel decisions
I give myself to God who has led me this far, and handled everything for me
Letting go, I am able to forgive, I am able to believe

Obvious signs tell the tale,
And yet taking secret time to notice
I stumble upon new meaning
On a timeline that seemed so hopeless

A new perspective gained from
A return to my roots,
The playground of my first school
From me has yet to be removed

And the message is quite clear
Using divine semiotics
For the irony blatantly appears
Through psychological tectonics

A great shift is upon us
And my microcosmic life
Is the harbinger of such
Like an eruption in the night

From deep in my self conscious
Comes a spilling forth of raw material
Ethereal visceral lava launches
Forth an epiphany so painfully real

I get my prescription of greendom
From a soul from my youth
And he still happens to reside ironically
Under the exact same roof

Across from the school
Where I first met rejection
I still wait like a fool
To meet my old weed connection

And it's true that we've puffed
In high times and rough
We've become bros and been through some stuff
But I'm starting to feel like enough is enough

My blackened lungs wheeze
As they beckon me to try
To finally set my soul at ease
And to that playground say goodbye

And I stop and think of the lost
The older brothers who were swallowed in the darkness
And I think of the painful cost
And the passion that went unharnessed

And then there's me and my buddies
After ten years slipped by
Sittin' back with our nuggies
Wasting days and staying high

And now the paradox confronts us
To leave the schoolyard haze
And the sundried memories of fun
Or squander our few days

And then another vision on the hill
The tower now prominent still
But dreams of the big screen
Are still to be fulfilled

But first things first
Says the bringer of the sign
Whether blessed or cursed
We will know in future rhyme

Childhood must now be shed
My life cycle has made a turn
And Jesus knows I begged and pled
And for my toys I burn

A man must climb up out of here
And into a new dawn
I've been at recess year after year
And I've stayed for far too long

O<small>H</small> <small>BITTER CONSTELLATION</small>, love is the secret that we all know

Only in Cali could there be gold nugget like me buried
Beneath the competitors and good looking ones
Who die to go first and kill to be noticed
I am the tortoise who wins the human race

I know that good things are on the horizon because I can feel it
Beneath every living hell I've endured, lays a hope and a joy
A warm center that is fed by the night of non existence
And thus cannot be extinguished forever

So day in and day out
As I wade through the champions of Reality Show glory
Letting them all take their anger and hate out on me
I conquer the world, one step at a time

Simple is the secret I know, but hard to master it is
Let go and let God
Let God sort you out
Let God solve tomorrow's problems
Let God show you the way
Let God alleviate your suffering
Let God give you what you need

Only remember, that turning your back on the source
And seeking the things that are forbidden
Will cause you to fear for what consequence you've earned
And you will only morn the time you spent estranged

Only the one who can count the hairs on my head
Can truly know the depth of my grief
The layers of pain, and how many levels I am hurting on
The absolute desolation that's cold enough to test my beliefs

Unutterable is my alienation these days, so vastly alone
Scanning the wilderness for a comfort and a home
Carrying on like a man who died long ago
In this vacuous void I contritely roam

Always fighting against the strongest social tide
I'm losing ways to save my life
Living through the hell I've made, and all the years I've cried
Still waiting out the strife, still missing a wife

Born with a beast whose appetites abound
And feeding this beast must be done with means which are sound
Otherwise the consequences can be dire,
And one can easily be plunged into the eternal fire

Could she be my mysterious one, in ways I can imagine
Could my love for her be stirred in methods so grim and tragic
I must find my path and allow and love all that is and will be
As the window of time reveals the universal wisdom and magic

OOOWW,OOHHH,AHHA
The blade stabs and stabs
The truth slices at my being

Not only am I not demonstrating any kind of
X-games prowess, I have failed socially
Both in physical appearance and behavior.

The girl I truly love and wish I
Could be with has rejected me utterly
And I officially have no self-esteem

I am you're whipping boy
Abhorrent filth reviled
Failure is my identity

Our society has descended into chaos because of sports
And war is the extension of it.
A fascist institution that breeds men like beasts
And instills a spirit of competition

I played sports because it's what daddy taught me
But I became quickly disillusioned with the contentious mentality
The egotistical displays, the barbarism, the rationality of it all
Striving to beat others goes against my religion

Golf is cool because you can just play the course
Surfing can be cool because it's just you and the wave
But unfortunately the scarcity mentality of striving
Pervades the calm and peaceful waters when it's crowded

Fascist physicality, fascist separationism, we are all one
The leaf doesn't yellow without the silent knowledge of the tree
And the egoism that is derived from this culture
Causes schism amongst the people, which we send out to the world

America is constantly parading its athletes around
And yet thinkers are seldom extolled in such a way
Everything has become so physical, so immediate
And the problem doesn't stop off the field.

We have become a culture of societal athletes
Earning money and purchasing cars that speak of status
Having surgeries to make us look more American
And obtaining empty things frivolously

And now we have a Commander in Chief who has an athletic view of the presidency
The kind of guy who loves football because of the hard hits
There's winners and losers, and the winners play the game the best
And the losers, well they can one day be winners too, if they just keep playing

But I don't play the game, I don't want your game
You can't turn me into a mindless drone carrying out menial tasks on a field or court somewhere

Yeah I flipped on my skateboard, yeah I caught a big wave
The whole world searching for external gratification

And so we have descended into this chaos, and millions have been consumed
The fascist athletic institution has pitted you against your brother
And now you chase a carrot that doesn't fulfill
And all you win is a reason to look down on others

Overcoming is a joy that is warranted in Heaven.
The greater climbs are the most fulfilling, and rewarding
Thus the hopeless wanderer who finds his true self is
Granted greater fire to compel their joy
For they have truly endured and can properly revel in the sweetness
In order that they may use it against the sadness of the loss
And letting go of the difficult things
Makes one able to overcome the equal challenge again
As does that pilgrim forge a path
That can be traversed by one who might follow.

I'M SMILING INSIDE because I've mystified myself again with my imagination.
What is this construct we brew, what form, what telling, what worth?
Is it because I stayed too long at the gate that the vision of what I could have been haunts me
I consider this to be the grueling chore.
 How do I make imagination and reality come into perfect semblance and order?
How do I achieve what I can conceive of?
Only that which has constructed all of my being
Can inform me of such wondering?
My self hatred is placated by the heart and the demon.
Moved against myself in an erosion of hope
As wretched as I've been, I cannot be denied
And as much as I burn with self humiliation and regret
Frustration and infuriation, discouragement and rejection
Utterly constant agony, the only time I elude pain is when I am stimulating myself with some
sort of Sensual pleasure or escaping into a dream in which I lose myself in my imagination.
Blessed to live in beautiful places, but unable to enjoy myself,
Unable to love myself every step of it.
What is it like to be happy?
What must life be like for those who don't struggle inside constantly
All of my blessings are squandered it seems,

But I can't be killed off

Paralyzed this time, I crawl forward with great strain
Like a storm is this coldness, like gravity this pain
Thinking back with grief and regret, devastated every day
Forever winter, with brief relief, from fires shared with slaves

Smacked down by a thought so woeful it drops
A torn soul to a new floor and the chill never stops
Perhaps I shant wake to see a new day this time
Perhaps I am closer than ever, and I only fear that I'm left behind

Undeniably though I am tragically flawed, a pity that I bear
This weighty life upon my back and no one seems to care
I can't blame people for how they take me, the problem is in me
There's nothing that can be done, no one who can set me free

Snowflakes fall as I see my life alone, a shallow bitter end
And somewhere in my heart of stone, I feel it break again
A part of me will soon be dead, and then shall never mend
As I seek my final resting place with no lover and few friends

PEOPLE SHOULD BE made to feel good about themselves
Especially kids.
Teachers, parents and peers wanted me to fit in
I never did.

Filled with self doubt I was dissed and abused daily
I can't win
I never wanted to play the game and do what I was told
Or get pigeon holed in

I chose to be honest and I intimidated them all
I'm never in
But what they did to me year after year made me sick
It's such a sin.

PERFECT IS subjective
Perfect silky shiny hair
Perfect skin lips and tits
Perfect ass, cock, physique

So often the word is defined by the beast
A two dimensional god
A media monster
A criteria put forth on a screen

Girls dying to be skinny enough
Shaven boys performing childish tricks
Catching footballs and waves of despair
Doing what they are told, striving to fit the mold

Forged by the religion of the new millennium
A television deity that reigns supreme over our lives
Permeating daily life and collective consciousness like an infernal wind
Beckoning those desperate for attention and acceptance

And what of those who accomplish the grim deed
What do they attain really?
A state of contention unceasing
A state of pretension unyielding

And the nasal whiny stuck up tone of the girls that fit
And the immature insecure tough guy dis of the dudes who play
And the result is a mean culture, cold as a blade
And a recipe for disaster

For why should they think?
When they get done selling their soul to make the grade
Scratching and clawing their way there, fucking over anyone
Only to be vacuous at the top of the game, ruler of the lame?

It's misery all around, everything everywhere sucks
If it has anything good left at all it is being used up

If it was good it's played out and beat
And everyone is way too self conscious to create anything worth while

Artists that did good stuff before are paraded around
So much they literally die before our eyes
And not just art, our government, our culture, our planet
Our lives are being eroded right before our agonized eyes

And everyday the television god comes into our homes
And lies to us each night telling us how pretty it all is and good
A fictional reality somehow depicted, commercials delineating a consumptive narrative
The power of suggestion, live like this and you'll be fine

Oh you're depressed, here take a pill
Nothing ugly exists here
Britney's happy can't you tell
She's perfect and you should be like her!!!

Perhaps, once, I figured my impetus
To change was enough to save me
But suddenly I realize that change
Is synonymous with survival

Change me, enhance me, make what needs to be
In order that I might survive
Let me yearn to survive
And not falter in my will
To continue, to live

I'll flow like a beautiful ocean
Alone yet interwoven
My lifeline is residual love
The essence of what should have been
I will define my love

Saving grace that is love, my only truth
Tell me how you work you're magic
So I am reassured, so that I might stay
I wish to stay, but the pain is all too much

Scattering my lifeless body to the ruins
Enduring cold torture at the hands of truth
I am terrified at the way I destroy myself
Then I think of how love and I are eternal
And I'm seriously warmed and reassured

RATHER THAN GETTING BETTER the walls are merely closing in
I thought wrong when I figured I would matter
Either they would come around or throw me in the bin
Time is proving that it will always be the latter

From the get go I have been thrown away to die
My reality is the leftover crap they didn't want
Now I find myself wondering why I should even try
Nowhere to call home, this forgotten world I haunt

I just get to work on bettering myself in pain
Pick up my bruised ego and swallow my pride
I feel as though I'll never wake up happy again
Carrying on though it seems I've already died

Now I sleep in my angry bed with nightmares
Failing at enlightenment and Christianity
My broken heart beats on yet nobody cares
And I'll wake up tomorrow to more calamities

Everyone who's ever gotten to know me has left me
They see the struggle I endure and want no part of it
Through my tears I try to promise them I'll be free
They may understand my sad plight but never love it

Athletes and soldiers are much more heroic than me
I just go on day by day in this mental captivity
Years go by and I keep dreaming that they'll see
That I am an amazing person in solid slavery

But no one can take up the burden of my love
I sure can't, thus loneliness eternal
The pain of flesh and blood that I begrudge
Is a symptom of the fiery Inferno

Without worth I can't appreciate myself at all
If to them I am futile I can't have hope
And without any hope the weight makes me fall
And I'm buried like the sacred antidote

RIGHT NOW SOMEWHERE someone is being saved
Someone just had a thought that rescued them from despair
Somebody just felt that wind of recognition of God's love
Somebody just took that breath that assures them they aren't sick anymore
Someone just saw the light at the end of the tunnel
And this moment is infinite!

Satan has taken my dreams from me this far in life
I am weak in the knees and have grounded my flight
Stumped by my addictions and frozen in a holding cell
I am an observer watching the world go down to hell

There's so much that my heart wishes to say and do
And so much passion that's trapped under the morning dew
So many nights like this living in my imagination
Running away from the painful truth of my stagnation

All I can do is rise again and crawl until tomorrow
And find a way to grow out of this consuming sorrow
My ambition is sapped by a demon in my breast
And my enduring will is again put to the ultimate test

Will I find the wisdom and the strength to save my own soul?
Or will this demon have its way and these sins take their toll?
I give myself to God who has been there all along
Beckoning me to obey him and stop being so wrong

So now my mornings are stained with regret
And my dreams are full of things not accomplished yet
But miraculous is my lord and savior
And he can rescue me from this demon forever more

Satan whispers into the ears
Making us believe his lies
He speaks to us of fears
He hopes each of us dies

All of these voices are false
The rantings of the fallen third
And every day that beckoning call
In each of us can be heard

It takes a large heart to gain this wisdom
One that has been through hell and back
One must be able to discern in which voice to listen
To drive this fucker home after another Satan attack

The hero drives the day to perfection
And each and every need is fulfilled
And his faith will bring ten million resurrections
And yet a deeper knowing is instilled

Semiotics prevents me from becoming demystified,
When I make meaning from the signs
A girl protesting for more girl power fuels a lie
And when I search for abuse on TV
Instead I found a message sublime

She's carving a bigger gulf of schism between her and me
And leading me toward a lower destiny
I would like to see a move toward unity
Cause when I got home again on my knees
I looked with hate to TV

And the message was from a preacher, with real sincerity
Telling me to solve the problems with rooted fidelity
And the message is wrapped in obscene irony
As is the message on the shirt from the social authority
You look down on **me**!

She kicked hard against her closing eyes
To excited to say goodbye to this night
But the spirit of dreams came down the alley
Under the orange moon as it rose over the rooftops

And then I slipped into a dream of my own
I went to the same sleep that I have succumbed to before
Though my eyes were open, I drifted into oblivion
Only a different spirit visited me down the alley a little further

A whisper on the wind that reminded me of what I was
The moon had turned pale white, and glared at me
And I trembled at the thought of all I stood to lose
Should Mr. Hyde continue to emerge

The sanctuary is abandoned in pursuit of the essence
The delectable enticements of the flesh
Lead us into cauldrons of boiling fate
And we say what the hell

But the child within us all is the hero in the end
Rising us up from our slumber just in time to catch the train
Off into the sunset of eternity, the last train to salvation
Only to proclaim God's mercy to those on board

She lives and breathes, it makes it real
The self hate I feel
God forgives but TV doesn't
And you and I still both agree

I'm messed up, a cluttered fool
I would have loved you
And supported you're every quest
Even beyond the tomb

I understand that holds no weight
I realize I have no value
And as drug addiction tugs on my sleeve
I suffer a terrible explosion anew

A thought beyond contempt
A dream unkempt
A torture chamber
A forgotten leper
A life unloved
Forgotten self
Invoking the end
Yet clinging on
Alive yet dead
I never mend
And I cannot hold onto friends

And I freeze and suffocate at night in bed
And I yearn for someone to caress my face
A face that I could love, one that I'm happy to give
And a sex that was clean and good, yet I am a disgrace

How can I erase my past? How can I clean the glass?
When will I know the taste of love upon my mass
I was tricked into a staining dirge
That I sang when I was really young
How am I to love what I am?

It sounds like I'm the one ruled by TV
But I just realize we all are
And this generation has deemed me unqualified for love
What I am merely can't be tolerated in America

Fortunately I believe I am eternal and I'll return again
I'll live again, and again in fact, like the dream of my tarnished youth
Jesus came and whispered in my child mind
Forever is a real long time

Exhilarating
Enchanting again and again
It never ends
What is blackened will mend
In this lifetime or next
If we forgive ourselves
We will rise up out of hell.

She said she loves being with me but I still gots to go
She tries to make future plans but I'm right out the do'
I belong to the night and to the night alone

And I will sit and bewail the ones who were lost before
The suicides of the past, the despaired and the forlorn
We belong to the night and to the night alone

Taking handfuls of acid and guzzling booze and drugs
They ask us why we do this and are met with honest shrugs
We belong to the night and to the night alone

Shooting our wads and burning our bridges, we wander
We speak of demise and its death that we ponder
For we belong to the night and to the night alone

Beyond this clay vessel, we long for our true home
And lonely as we are, we hurt everyone we know
We belong to the night and to the night alone

And as the day comes to a close
I embrace this pain only they will know
Alas I belong to the night and to the night ALONE.

SHOULD IT BE THAT I waste away
And suffer this each and every day
Alone for this life, alone to stay
I can always get down on my knees and pray

That the beatific ladies at the rivers mouth
Will dip me in the water and cleanse my self doubt
And all of this suffering and pain will dissolve
And around our Father we will revolve

It's not my parents fault and no one on TV
And it's not what you have it's what you are
And I've been rotten from the beginning
And unfortunately deeply scarred

Oh mystical journey forever beckoning
Leaving me here in bitter questioning
I don't deserve you're mercy yet beg it
I must enter now the river of regret

SLAVERY, SLAVERY, SLAVERY, how long will you last!
Will I be delivered, or is all surely lost
Grim nights, overcome, embarrassing ordeals
Devastated over and over again, I am afraid, and torn.

Liquid reality, I flow through unannounced
I drag myself past you trapped in a mind
Impossibly pronounced is my dilemma
I know that there is never no light

Leper head, He can only heal
The one that scanned the furthest reaches of the darkness
The one that lead the way to lasting peace
Beyond life into Life, eternal

Smacked in the face of my pride
My name will be mud, I'm sure
Crusty memories of who I was
The sickness is all they know of me

My treasures always placed in a hiding place
Only I can find them, and only I will enjoy them
I fear terribly that my liberation will be isolated
I see no other way, but then I cannot foresee the ways of the One

Oh merciful life force that we call the ALL
Oh giver and mover, redeemer and punisher
Liberate my soul from these binds, lift us up from this bondage
Please Oh Heavenly light, set the angels in us free.

LIBERTY

Small token of my devotion to a dream, distant rewards hold me steadfast to my goal.

To cap off my journey I need just one last reminder of what I need to sacrifice.

I need to taste the painful bliss until it is implanted indelibly upon my regretful conscience.

Could the world be simply waiting for me to attend their birth, the revelation of the soul, the awakening of the deepest heart, immaculate.

Small am I in virtue and in deed, stepping brazenly over stagnant and familiar ground.

"Come on", they say, go to where you need to be and set us all free.

So HOMOGENIZATION took place from the silver screen
And that affected all of our mentalities
And what that screen told you and me
Helps me understand why I'm **unseen**!

So this is what love feels like
This might be my first good day I've ever had
It turns out that love doesn't equal joy
It doesn't suddenly feel warm inside
I merely have the will and the strength
To get back up after being kicked
In the teeth for the millionth time

How dare I call this my dream
Not a big cock or wallet
Not a big wave or fat air
Not rock stardom or literary success
I merely wanted to walk under the moon
Without the constant shame I've felt
Or cooking up more bad karma

I feel my brain draining
All the tar and toxins
Are being processed by my being
I'm never turning back
I have to become the saint
I've been reluctant to become
It's the only avenue to peace

My lust is drying up again
A rivulet of blood that has flowed
Since my early childhood
My anger is turning to power
After being thrown away for good
And now approaches my finest hour
I will finally be understood

Somehow the pain ceased momentarily
And it is in that interim
That we must search for it
What life must be like for some who are
Not consumed

I cannot find any way to alleviate this suffering
I just can't understand why
Some lives aren't plagued like me
And there is so much contention in the world
I am swept away

What is it like to be free, from yourself?
My two afflictions still grow
Further into error I/we go
With a fear and skepticism that can't be helped
No reason why!?

Repent again and beg for mercy eternally
A corrupted youth still lost
What good are my dreams
When there's a lifetime between me and them
And all that time is gone

Sometimes a soft rain falls upon my happiness
And my peace is invaded with a wretched knowing
Like a blood stain that cannot be washed away
A truth that can be forgiven but not forgotten

This culture that we love and extol
Has left me looking inside for my entire life
Alone and alienated by kids, teachers
Bosses, counterparts and celebrities

A nation that chooses a few that conform
And casts aside those who question it
Has left me alone and discarded like second class refuse
And now the years have run together

And I have to keep striving to not become a hater
Not to spit back at those who have spit on me
I am a rebel forever on the outside
Futility my only enemy, ineffectuality it's ally

Utopia, it has been speculated
Consists of Capitalistic Individualism
Infused with just the right amount of Altruism
So that the people are at once free and loved

But America is a dystopia
Where decadence reigns supreme
And happiness is fleeting
And the wrong few are lifted

And those who move upward
Are chased through their tragic lives
By angry probes that aim to destroy
That which found a way to thrive

But I remain cold and unwanted
Intimidating to those who have compromised and strove

I remained simple and honest, unpretentious and without ambition
In the face of cultural excommunication and ostracization

And it is entirely possible that I will not be allowed
By myself or those who decide who will rise
To flourish and be a cultural force to be reckoned with
And live and die here in the forgotten outside

Sorrow will forever be a part of my life
Self sabotage and a life of strife
Born onto this sinking ship
And I have to rekindle the dwindling light

Arrogance and shame have claimed my love again
Taken from the morning and the day is lived in pain

A damaged second hand good
I still won't do what I should
Promising this my one last trip
A promise I would keep if I could

I don't blame them when I'm thrown away
A lifetime of this and I'm now insane
Crossing the threshold time after time
No rational methods will remove this stain

Deep wounds that never heal, and now fresh one's on top
Unless I make this change finally it's never going to stop

Each new sin a harbinger for disgrace
Both then and now I'm locked behind my face
Standing stiff, I'm rigid and repressed
I am frozen to the bone in this deep and empty space

Crawling towards the future like those who are left behind
It's no wonder now it seems that I don't trust my mind

Yet somehow I feel stronger here today
Perhaps it's because I no longer fear the pain
And should I die one of these dark nights
Know that I'll feel right at home when you bury my remains

Sᴛᴀʀᴛ ᴛᴏ sᴇᴇ ᴛʜᴇ ᴡᴀʏ you were formed, the way you were led astray and the way you were allowed to fester.
There's no finger to point no ambition to blame and no difference to claim.

Crawl with me until we find some shelter in a hole or some stranger's arms.

Smile inside because you see beyond the truth, you see beyond life, beyond death, and beyond good and bad.

Beyond rot and healing. Within an ocean that envelops us all, yet not all can perceive. Attain emptiness in your home,

And stay where you are firm, thus you will find your hidden treasure, the components for all you will ever need.

Cast away your isolation as a means of knowing thy self. Let the desires melt into a river of thought and be dissolved by the rotation of the All.

We are all one mind, one consciousness, yet we flow at different rates and in a myriad of streams, but all to the same ocean, our true home, our serenity.

Sᴛᴀᴛɪᴄ ᴀᴄʜɪᴇᴠᴇᴍᴇɴᴛs, ɪɴᴇꜰꜰᴇᴄᴛɪᴠᴇ in the broader scheme of things, I have no regard for me, I'm not willing

I DON'T UNDERSTAND God's will. I just can't seem to let things be. I feel like I'm missing something, letting myself down, wasting my life. I just can't seem to validate my plight, I just can't dignify my being

How come some are beautiful, some are attractive, some are nice, some are fun to be with, some are loved?

Yet some are tested, or challenged, basically rejects?!

Rejected and overlooked, allowed to live and even encouraged to thrive, but contained in the silent understanding that you simply aren't capable of being considered an equal. No success when it comes to the personal life, a plight relegated to acceptance. Some swallow humility and some forever refuse it.

Truth be told I can't say that I can truly let go of my wounded ego, I don't think I can stand below you.

I have never learned that I am acceptable as a human

Steal away the happy air, you crusty vacuum of despair
Call me back to my dark roost just as the sun is rising to scare
The tumbling worries into their hiding abodes,
And simmering the raging hordes
And yet still from my wintry cell do I desperately stare.

Call me home you just ministers, you dark lords
Set me upon my unhappy helm and watch me lead the scores
Of ailing souls, trapped in eternal restraint
Down the river of blood, through the valley of hate
It is my place, my purpose and divine incorporeal chore.

Smiles dissolve like clouded sun-beams, swiftly forgotten
Fearful whispers remind me that I'm rotten
Doomed to lead this charge, until the end
To those unfortunate enough to be around I lend a hand
We persist like the damned must, learning to love in the piss we fought in.

Resolution soothes us not, fine weather leaves us burned
Fine things slip through our bloody hands, a million times scorned
Come watch me if you dare, A graceful ghost I am
I take your warmth and leave you feeling bland
Because the legend I promised still hasn't returned!

Still rotting and living in fear eh?
Striving then diving back to the bottom of the sea
A rip current that I just won't fight
Pinned down here where the darkness envelopes me

Every time I get up and try
I turn and lay back down
And when people see my bedsores
As I stroll through town
They dismiss me to the darkness
That I have always called my own.

I'M FALLING OVER MYSELF, lookin' for creature comfort at the ultimate price
And once again I've spoiled paradise, once again I can't suffice
Crawl away again, this nightmare never ends, stay out in the rain
"Get yourself together", move forward til' the end, endure the pain

Frail is my heart, endangered is its love, lost in the cold nights
Where is she Mother? I can't seem to dig up the light
This blackness is overwhelming, I can't see anymore
Tears fall in vain time after time, a million more in store

Death is not an out, I must find my way to her, time is not the issue
Call on me please, come rescue me because I miss you
I've thrown away life a million times over, love has driven me to crack
I've set forth on a course and God knows there's no turning back

Demise, demise, demise, all my years in waste caught up to me
I'm not even running anymore, I embrace the pain contritely
I will have to turn my face from the fire now, into the depths I stare
Chilled, I shiver in my bones, my heart and soul are bare

Close your eyes and feel love leak away from you until you cave in
Crawl to your post and stand watch among the lonely slave kin
We are all just whispering through the universe of strife, begging to be released
Are you fighting a solemn war on an internal front? Will my life ever know peace?!

When doubt sets in and faith is tested, miracles are born in the void
Only those who keep their watch doth hell avoid.

THE AMERICANS OF 2009 are twisted in a way the world has never seen
The Market has frozen and the insects have been lulled to sleep
The competitors have assumed their superficial roles
And a technological beast has emerged from the murky deep

A media giant has invaded all of the free living space
Informing the masses of their standing in the rat race
Like a vengeful serpent out to destroy us all
He hides his malice beneath a good looking face

He brainwashed our leaders who have become self obsessed
He alienated our lovers who've been rendered dispossessed
The truth was absconded by this perpetrator of ill
But it was in the end revealed to those who confessed

To be honest these days is to withdraw from the game
Let go of unending desperation for fame
Please God not the humans who've tuned black from the screen
Their sleek perfect bodies chiseled with shame

THE BATTLE IS HARD fought today
I lost again in my own way
But should the grace of God remain
I'll live to fight another day

I collapse under the heat
I hold fast and then retreat
Like Augustine I have a chain
And I am prone to repeat

The wretched sins of my past
I wonder how long this will last
The pollution of my youth has left a stain
And I better clean it up fast

Lest I invoke the wrath of the Lord
In which case hell's in store
A lingering, simmering pain
To taunt me evermore

But I digress
I can clean my mess
I must now wait in the rain
To be blessed

The birth of Rock and Roll was kinda' lame
I mean Buddy Holly, Chuck Berry and Elvis are pretty cheesy overall
Then the Beatles came along, and their early shit was pretty gay
But then came some pretty gnarly shit from them and the Stones
But the Doors blew the doors off all the shit

Jim lived in his music spiritually, and profoundly
And so did Led Zeppelin and Pink Floyd
And they traversed a new path into existence
And spawned some worthy offspring along the way
Namely the Offspring

And Guns n' Roses and Metallica marked the end of an era
They watched the decline with helpless eyes
Ozzy fathered those who heralded in the end
Marilyn and Tool brought us to Eminem somehow
And for now it's only the same old voices shouting from lonely rooftops

And these bands carry the legacy on with exasperating diligence
But this new generation is all but devoid of spiritual inspiration
Even Christian rock is as painful as Creed was
A wave of sizzling temporality has washed over the entire universe
And those few who still possess souls that are awake know

How daunting is our future task, how to wake these people up
From their slumber of competition and egoism
From there greedy schemes and self absorbed ambitions
From pretentious status recognition
Then and only then shall rock and roll live again

The challenger stares the future in the face
He lets go and becomes visceral, eluding viscosity
Climbing, climbing, like the salmon up the stream
He flows through the stagnant waters into a new reality

A daunting task is the one we all know well
We can calculate the difficulty in degrees
Down in degrees into each stiff breeze
The poet flows scantily through hell

Climb a new arch and make an offering
An invocation of God, a sacrifice to Him
To let him know that you know he knows you
To give it up in faith, to know eternal gifts await

THE CHURCHES MAY be full on Sunday
But the soulful one's are few and far between
And the number is decreasing day by day
As the world fills up and becomes more mean

The population rise and the race for TV health
Has caused the race to become divided
And each competes against the other as we consume ourselves
And we abandon collectively the civilization we relied on

The demon, the one I've always known
Sits and waits in me where he is right at home
Knowing my reluctance to deny
He's trying to corrupt me through my mind

I turn to Christ like an old faithful friend
And look to him still begging him to mend
I have to wage a war with my self
Or truly this inner darkness will only spread

Like the prodigal son coming back home to life
And the tomb of Jesus filled with white light
The golden hearted warrior will triumph
Over the seas of darkness and the deadly night

THE FEELING WENT AWAY, the gloom and doom that stole the sun
And it was because I had to hear from someone else
Someone who seemed to feel the same
Those who are on the outskirts like me
And relief came from an unlikely place, TV

Maybe it was due to the fact that I had pulled up the anchor
And drifted on the current of sin that previously had done me in
But when I awoke the world reeked like a rotten carton of milk
Left in the fridge and begging to be discarded
And somehow tonight shines in a way that hasn't occurred in years

As I drove to Burger King to devour animals I know lived tragic lives (and met painful tragic deaths)
I passed hordes of Catholic illegals pouring out of the Mission
Pushing strollers of doom and representing the dying American ideal
Accompanied by white trash whose ignorance lends to despair
And I got in a downright shitty mood

And by the time I got to Target and the little Emo chick flailed
And couldn't tell me how much room I had left on my card
And a kook at the disgusting laundry mat I'm forced to do my laundry at
Took up two places and slammed his door into the side of my wife's car
I thought I might actually be looking into those anti depressants on the commercials for clones

But as I returned home and turned on the television I usually loathe
A voice screaming in the wilderness appeared
George Carlin did a stand up performance that saved me from my melancholy
He basically stated the deepest sentiments of my soul
By maintaining a level of disgust with humanity that I needed to hear

And when he declared that he fantasized about natural disasters morphing
Into tragedies of a biblical scale
My soul was soothed and my mood changed
And I knew I wasn't alone on earth
Cringing at the state of humanity and wishing it would just hurry up and end

Then I watched the South Park movie
And it brought me higher
And it seemed as though it was the only thing on Television that needed to be viewed
With over 500 channels of crap to choose from
South Park will present one with all they need to keep up with today's farcical reality

And just to make the night really meaningful
VH1, which I usually loathe with the same fervor I reserve for MTV,
Did a chronicle on the history of Heavy Metal
And reminded me that there are those who still yearn for better days
Whose laments and outrage ease the souls of those still "trapped under ice"
After thirty long dry thirsty years on this beautiful planet, held captive by this wretched race.

The heart carries you through
The weight of the world can't extinguish the light
The limbs can be broken
The will tested and even squelched
There is a cup that is never exhausted

The greatest sacrifice was paid by Him
That paid the horrific price
The cost of my ticket was paid
So that I could witness the spectacle he had performed
For the blind who demanded to see

But there is a piece within that comes from above
A force that compels beyond time
And though the trials of life can do us in
Something inside carries us home
And our completion can be achieved

Many have endured the evil of others
And some may truly have someone to blame
But we are told to love and forgive
To think outside of time and beyond ourselves
To think eternally and carry on as such

THE LOVE OF SIGNS draws me forth
The mythological, the magical
All are part of this bumpy course
Through the everlasting battlefield

Miracles and ghosts save us from our hardships
They carry us on high and hold us there
And should we fall again our saving starlets
Will heed our desperate prayers

Like the wind that blows a seed to take root
A message arises in my consciousness
I am an integral part of the manifestation
Thanks to our Creator's graciousness

And into tomorrow I slide and glide
Wondering how the magic will be my guide
Beyond reason is my savior, and trusting I'll abide
To the forces that the Instructor sends forth from inside

Following this golden light within
Reaching out to end my sins
I find myself warmed within
By the loving hand of mercy
That sees beyond the people we've been

THE MAN ON THE streets told me it was simply cat and mouse
He isn't wrong

THE QUALITY OF life has been
Gradually declining since the late eighties
Ever since then we began to sizzle
And seal ourselves off from each other more and more
A Post Modern digitized existence

And we can't expect things
To get better immediately
Considering the population is exploding
And the green revolution is mired
And the truth is obscured to the rational mind

There needs to be a dramatic shift
Globally and locally
An entirely new way of envisioning
Living here on earth with one another
Harmoniously, productively and joyfully

The way we travel from one place to another
Exposes the root of the problem
Angry people racing their cars down freeways
Completely incapable of mere courtesy
Making our way down the wide open roads

Always upset at the crowds and yet they still grow
Millions of lost sailors, tossed by infernal winds
Lifestyles and possessions, surface perfection
There is a vacuum that needs to be filled
The world is just sitting around waiting for a revolution

The stage has been set for egoists to beat their chests
And promise to be violent if it comes down to it
But the revolution is going to have to be one of love
One way or another the universe shall be righted
Will we live to see it is the million dollar question

People need to fulfill God's will and fear Him as well
In his mercy he allows all of this separation
But the faithful always rest within, warm and calm
Knowing that the Almighty will have His good will be done
They ride the river right through death into eternity

The rise of Atheism
These dudes pissed off at God
Claiming Jesus boned Mary Magdalene
There's no Noah's Arc
They all think God resembles Fallwell

Interesting name for him in fact
He died just after claiming God had removed his protection from America
Careful with that tongue Eugene
I don't think abortions are cool either
But we all live with sin

But the backlash caused by small people on other small people
Now the History channel and Discovery channel
Refute God's existence
In order to make the godless, scared atheists
Rest a little better

But to the faithless rationalists
Comes no peace on earth, never any understanding
They remain sealed in spiritual darkness
The light cannot penetrate their dim wit
No matter how learned they become

Sure God gave us the faculty of Reason
So that we might tend to our dominion
Responsibly and prudently
But because the scientists stopped believing in God
Our Reason has become futile and our dominion failing

Now as the earth suffers at our hands worse than ever
And believing in God is as unpopular as Michael Jackson
And all this talk about whether or not we derived from the beast
The beast is within us, and we are capable of becoming it
And it manifests in various ways

The one inside of me begs for satiation
And I chill it out with copious amounts of weed
Or cigarettes or alcohol
Anything to squelch the desire
We must subdue our inner beast

That is where we are separated
From our non human co-inhabitants
We are taught to not become the beast and be civilized
The capacity to love is common to all life on earth
And it's all the science one truly needs

God smiles and whispers into the heart of the true believers
He restores their faith each and every time it runs dry
From a perpetual fountain springing forth eternally from him
And with him we go off into the sunset each night
Unscathed by the nightmares dreamed up by the rational mind
The scientists always fail to see the entire truth
For if we can both agree that you and I both have souls
Than we must rationally conclude that there is an element of existence that is of a spiritual nature
And this element cannot be accurately taken into account
Unless those who try to explain the phenomena unfolding in our universe
Are able to ascertain and observe that which is not easily discerned
The elements that make up things like the heart and the soul and God
Do you think that when Jesus was killed his spirit did not live on
Are we merely our flesh and thus when it is exhausted we cease to be in every sense

Doctor's will not be able to cure modern plagues unless these laws are acknowledged
They must be incorporated and assimilated made a part of our cannon
It must be irrefutable by every stretch of reason that there is a spiritual element to existence in our perceived universe
Therefore next time you are afflicted
And you turn to blind reason for a cure
Don't be surprised when the remedy is ineffective
Or you only find temporary relief from your symptoms
Instead look deeply within your heart and ask yourself how you are living
Find out where you disobey your heart and discontinue those things
Or persist at them and see that the symptoms persist

The condition of our souls reflects the condition of our bodies
Would Superman's wife have perished if he was alive and strong?
Can you not overcome all adversity and physical malady?
If you tend to the soul which is the life spirit of that self same flesh
Make the soul warm like a healing oven
Feel the healing essence surrounding you into each moment
Observe scientifically and rationally, the irrational works of the spiritual world

"THE WORLD on fire"
Sometimes I think I'd rather be a liar
Than be in this mire

Addicted to TV
You think you're better than me
And it all comes down to looks and money

Born in to hell and told to climb out
Lonely and singled out
And a whole lifetime of drowning in self doubt

The girls say they want a guy with self confidence
But how can I feel secure when I'm so ominous
Living in sin and truant from divine providence

It keeps stacking up on top of me
And you wonder why I'm so top heavy
I'm poisoned, afraid and it all just looks ugly

Taking out my lust on my lungs and my heart
I've been aggravated by this assault
And I've survived despite being stricken from the start

There is no refuting miracles
From the good words I read truth
The cleansing that I need is spiritual
Let this demon be shaken from me

Looking back on nine years now
Don't ask me why because it's all a blur
Three years in Tahoe, where I hid out
Six years in hell, getting kicked to the curb

A beautiful nightmare, a collage of spectacles
Blank stares at the awesome mother
A myriad of faces and connections that mystify
Situations that seem to blend into one another

I followed a dream that came to me one day
And God's will saw it so
Visions from God, signs and words we hear, sing and say
The future has no pinpoint

The past was drawn out in a random succession
Lead by influence unknown
Impulses and addictions, favors and progressions
Sometimes just the urge to bone

People who are so there for one night
A million bridges burned
Scorched because you think it's right
Because from love we always turned

Born into wicked ways, a cycle hard to break
So much damage done so soon
Hope against hope for a time in which I'll wake
Lose myself in another tune

The solution seems out of reach now
But I know I'll find it

The secret still hasn't been found
The light still can't shine in

It is when I clear myself and walk right
That new dream will begin
And there's a good chance I'll be alone at night
But I can love again

THESE HEADPHONES seriously suck I swear
Today tried my patience to the bitter frail limits of the human heart
Some dude cut me off so I flipped him off, He told me I was
Young and dumb and happened to be right on

Some kinda' cute chick gave me her number in the bar tonight.
Even though I'm totally wasted, I had a pretty intelligible conversation with her.
And she actually demonstrated INTEREST in what I had to say.
And she's one of the more intelligent chicks out there
Thus, I might actually think about her.

Interlude from the real, escape from the frightening horror of my abominational self
Jesus blinds my eyes from time to time, but he can't really be serious, can he?
I'm crucified each day and yet he says turn thine other cheek.
Forgive those who have trespassed upon you,

But then again I'm tryin' to drop the habit of puttin' on the habit
It's a strange world Jesus
Go ahead torture me, break my heart and kill me
I forgive you

That's what he had to say,
That's what they did to him

She haunts my consciousness my Lord.
I frown on the thought of her immense beauty
I surrender to the fact that I am dead.
My love and my Christ
Shield me from these woes
The one I loved with all my heart was never even mine at all.

They say we live in the era of the knowledge explosion
But no one can agree on what the truth is
So instead of being better informed
We find ourselves collectively confused
And fighting

No wonder the Bible says that this will happen in the end
And the Anti Christ will take power over their minds
There's too many chefs in the kitchen
And they can't seem to agree on the simplest things
The groundwork

In a simpler time we could agree on certain things
And move forward knowing we were on the same page
But now our progress is stifled
By egotists desperate to be heard, desperate for money
We are mired

Science can explain certain things for sure
But of our origins they can only speculate
And they have yet to accurately predict the future
These things are for God alone to know
The scientists will be humbled

But wars will be fought over who is right
And many will die oblivious to the truth
Of diseases they thought had to kill them
For reason they thought they had to martyr themselves
Because they don't believe

And since they don't believe they become obsessed
With disproving the Bible and all that it says
They don't understand the words taken out of context
Their minds don't let them trust their hearts
In confusion they parish

So many avenues, so much stimuli
The mind is overrun with data and can never sort it out
The internet serves to only complicate the fragile sense of calm reason can muster
Most rationalists become disheartened and hardened
The heart alone will know

THEY TURNED INTO INSECTS, but why should I care
I mean I can totally see where they are heading
They want to go to places like Hollywood
They want to make a name for themselves

Problem is my culture has turned to Mammon worship
I saw it coming long ago
I mean I just separated myself from people and questioned everything all the way up
I am not like them

Athletes, paid billions because their anatomy is extolled like a god
Musicians who become priests of a shallow religion
Pitting one against the other
The seed is sown

California is consumed like a product
As seen on TV, people have come to the land of my youth
To become products themselves
And be sold on the international market

Hypothetical ideals; unreal, egotistical charades
Can you guess what I am being, I'm just like the commercial
I was this on a movie so I am going to live it
And obey my two dimensional God, hey whatever

Just quit fucking annoying the shit out of me
I don't give a fuck if you have stupid ass tattoos all over
Fucking hang out on Melrose, fucking be seen on a beach, do your thing
Just quit influencing my culture so much

I am so overwhelmed by these Godless ones
The flood must be near
But somehow despite their impressive breeding capabilities
And ability to consume

Me and mine will be just fine, all the days of our lives
And yours too, if you simply believe it

Enveloped in a loving hand
That prunes its trees, and uproots your weeds

And my Christian community, it repels me
I'm repulsed
But Christ's house is always open
And he is always in

And as I face another day where I literally take on the world
I am fed by a river of life
Beyond reason
I'm just lucky to be alive, and blessed with all I have

And whatever tomorrow brings, I'll try to love it
And when clones piss me off I'll let it be
And I won't be so mad at Eddie Vedder, or even Alanis and Jewel
Even though they broke my heart

Those who have a choice don't choose me
I'm a last resort human being

THROUGH THE VERY hole that I carved
I found a highway of bliss
And though somehow I am starved
I still feel a loving Godly kiss

I have chosen to indulge, I can't deny
And though Christ is much higher than I
I am tenderly reminded that I shall not die
And I only add weight making it harder to fly

My warm hands incubate my wedding ring
And my heart whispers it's rejoices
Despite smoking and excessive flagrant drinking
I am somehow above my earthly choices

I have demonstrated that I am willing to give a lot
For Christ, the Church, and any soul I trust
And my faith will prune me until I am free of rot
And my love will keep me from decaying lust

And it is true, I am afraid to bring this train into the station
And I linger in the comfort of my source
But this great hunger is a demon of my own creation
And I am pitied as one with no other recourse

Though I am dragged down by this learned behavior
Inside me resides a heroic advocate of just fate
And though I aspire to be an apostle for my Savior
I have to admit my conversion is coming quite late

Today offered the entire gamut
Emotions both sweet and horrible
I cursed the Lord in the afternoon stagnant
And found the evening so adorable

Saddam went to the gallows pole
And the world raised guns in protest or support
I feel ashamed to play the American role
In hate and anger the faces of the proud contort

Not only do I not agree with the war in Iraq
But I know that killing is never justified
And now the mistakes that have been made can't be taken back
And for even Saddam Hussein the angels cried

George Bush has claimed to believe in Christ
And his constituency is composed largely of the modern day Pharisees
But a killer with a crucifix emerged in the twilight
A harbinger of the coming night in which human harmony has ceased

The world has exploded into unbridled hatred
From the grocery store to the freeways to the news
Americans live like insects and hold nothing sacred
And each day of my life I am abused

With my heart on my shirt sleeve
I bravely step out into the battle of the parasites
Around the world this madness weaves
Palestine, Korea, India, and China erupt into a million fights

Bono lifts the night from the wreckage
"One" voice quieting the angry frenzied minds
And as the evil tide ominously beckons
Transcendence through his message one finds

And so in an instant one spends an eternity
Rising above the circumstances that beg us to hate
Finding a steely nerve from insecurity
The lamb and martyr has demonstrated how it is never too late

Tomorrow I've been a saint for fifteen years

Two LOVES I am blessed to have
Shone to me at once
A birthday blessing, two angels
Have joined in faith

A mother's sacrifice, a wife's cherished gift
Her body given as a sacrifice
Like Christ for the world
Her suffering and her will

And an angel as light as any there has ever been
Was brought forth from darkness
And peace descended upon the wilderness
And all the world smiled

I'm weary of the Republican Party
Mentality creeping up on me
Telling me to compete and kill
I don't feel the need to outdo others
Or try to determine how happy someone is

I fear the lack of a Democratic Party
And a leader strong enough
To guide the country off this collision course with destruction
That began a lifetime ago
During a Cold War and a regime change

I question the Ethics
Of getting someone to buy into your way
With broken promises and shallow lies
By intimidating people into buying your protection
From a foe that you created for this purpose

Aspiring to leadership for vain reasons
Has been the bane of human civilizations
Because takers will take if left unchecked
And when justice is corrupted the slightest bit
It festers into an abscess if not directly remedied

A father gave way to a son
Willing to do what it took to get in
Another fruit of his loins helped in Florida
And the contentious race was won
By a kook from Texas who was trying too hard to look like the man

Then either planned 911 or let it happen
In order to increase the power of the war god
With justifications for wire tapping to make us more unsafe
Only now not scared of some superficial artifice of an enemy
But made to feel intimidated by our own government

Remember, remember the 11th of September
Because the Republicans have hijacked the radio
And Fox news is broadcasting live to your home
With nervous broadcasters neurotically elaborating
Because the Republicans have a V for Vendetta bitch

I disagree with everything that's been done by the war Party
I could have masturbated all day to Internet porn in the oval office
Then smoked large amounts of confiscated weed
And lead this country to a glorious present
Full of hope and promise for the future

But the Democrats can't find their man
Liberal but not getting blown at work
Against the war but willing to concede some justifications
In order to not become marginalized
Story of my life

Always I am the one on the fringes
Driving through Amarillo Texas in my mind
Not able to fully jump on board with any of these trains running
And thus relegated to a social position just beyond reach
Where they can't touch me and yet I am ineffectual as well

And then in comes the jeering from the far right
Calling me a wuss because I don't seem willing to fight
Buying in to the obvious lies of their party
They drink beers and make points, I guess I can't argue
But something reeks to me and my nose always knows

So then the War Child fabricates justifications once again
And attacks a small country or two that suit his oil needs
To fuel his pathetic war machine that kicks ass
On littler ones like a fourth grade bully
With relative impunity because God blessed his forefathers

Then this kook let's a Hurricane turn into a harbinger
Of the bottled compassion of our leaders if this party continues its rule
Fixes another election with a little help from Ohio
And arrogantly leads the country into a mire in Iraq
And despite compromising civil liberties makes us all unsafe

If we can get the power back while there is still time
The world won't suffer further, and the damage can be reversed
But we need a collective shift from a fearful mind
The Republicans can see the future and it's well rehearsed
And this web they've weaved will take a while to unwind
They must be voted out before humanity is forever cursed

We Humans, we love magic
The rich want to possess it
The poor need it

We love to be more than we are
We love to know the mystical
And most of all, we need the love in it

We cry for it, we lie for it
We hope for it, and search for it
And most of us can't see it

We move by it, we're moved by it
We live with it, we dream with it
Some of us rely on it

But most of us scoff at it
We find it hard to believe in it
And in the end, we all remember it.

To attain it is the lie, to see it is the truth
To forget is to be blind, and to surrender is to know
And to smile is to witness

WE MAKE UP NAMES to call the ocean of pain
Sometimes it's an ex-girlfriend that never really was
Sometimes it's a political dichotomy that can't be solved
Sometimes it's name is poverty, disease or hunger
Sometimes it's a character flaw
Sometimes it's a physical attribute

Nomenclature to describe the suffering
The loss, the rejection, the frustration,
The agony, the longing, the cold
The lack, the mess,
The dark
Alone

We MUST RETURN NOW to that severed spring
To the land that hope was born in,
To the place where love glows like a whisper in your troubled mind,
Like a comet that struck somewhere long ago and there is no trace of the remnants
Of an event long ago, a mysterious enigma that has plagued our weary minds

We don't feel, we just don't feel, I don't like it one bit
We allow ourselves to be complacently amused by our frivolous illusions,
Weary am I of this condition, tired of the bland landscape

Take me home to a distant location, where prudence is unearthed within our soiled mistrusting existence
Take me far from here, like the cliché' says, I wanna' go home, (I'm whining)
I don't want to bombard my senses with the torrents of self-destruction any longer
I don't want to be left out here in the bitter cold where those who don't know love, wait!

We wait outside with our arms held close from the cold, like refugees we seek warmth in our humble abodes
Stupid as it sounds, I've invented new grounds, to justify my truancy
Crawling away from a beautiful day I found myself without a trace of life.

Smack me again for I deserve to be beat, I've ventured far and wide in the forbidden
Don't fuck me cause'   I am hurt, and I have no social life.
Don't get me wrong
You'll let me go because it's obvious that I need to die
I need to die and be born again within my own tired skin,
Without my dream goddess, my nightmare never ends.......

We need to bolster our self esteem
The benevolent Mother has different methods of incarceration;
The Earth Spirit said to the Mother
"That one is the Golden Child"
To which the benevolent Mother replied,
"We've lost ones like that before."

We'll be remembered by our debris
It's what the future ones will see
The disposable razors and plastic bottles
And oil in the sea

And our lives will be recounted on TV
And the future will see our grim stupidity
Clones, athletes and stuck up models
What not to be

And as I think about my new baby
I stop and think of how her world will be
Centered in her ancestors debacle
Inherent misery

WHAT A GREAT BAD day I had again
What an amazing journey trapped in myself
Everyday must be incredible for people in love
Cause I'm seeing so much beauty here in hell

From here in my searing roost
I have witnessed awakenings, rebirth, and glory
I saw an angel glorified by tooth
Tonight "trust in God" was the lead news story

I lie down in my burning bed and die
But yet live more than ever in a way
Damage done but still asked to try
Somehow today felt like a new day

Same fight and same sentence
But I smile at the stabbing pain somehow
Through faith and repentance
I can regain peace in the here and now

Loneliness feels so sweet tonight
This is truly as good as it's gonna' get here
Jesus may bless me beyond my dreams and expectations
But for tonight I'll have to be thankful for these sweet tears

What happened here in this place that I live?
This community, this society, this human race
The love has been lost, completely.

No one's walking around with any love in their hearts.
No one says hello to the people they encounter, unless they know them,
Unless they have deemed those people worthy of their attention or affections.

What kind of world do we live in anymore?
Frowny girls pass me by like I have the plague or something.
No one inquires about how or what I'm doing.

Everyone's so full of rivalry and contention
No one's reaching out to anyone anymore
Everyone's just out to get theirs and that's that.

The fig tree's branches have become tender, I can tell summer is here.
The great reckoning is upon us and we must hold fast to love.
A great die off is upon us and those who love will last.

WHAT HAVE WE learned from this,
Our escapades through time?
You think you're on it
Well I say that's fine

You call yourself healthy
And I say look again
From where I stand
You're all insane

Somehow something is coming to a close in me
I feel the natural passing of the course
My personal revolution will show how you're in need
Of a purging at the source

Look down on me as if you had an answer
Talk down to me as if you weren't the same
I won't smile 'til I change
Yet your smile is deranged.

Just stay away from me
Sure I'm the one who's lost
But you don't see yourself
Through the social holocaust.

America is fruitful if you're healthy and you're wise
If you're selected she will fuel you
But if you should be ill in head, and colored with demise
American society will disown you!

WHAT IF I CAUGHT AIDS one day
What if I just couldn't pay ------the rent
What if I dropped out of school
What if I didn't get out of bed

Would you still believe in me?!
Would you still believe in me, my Lord

What if I lost all my hair
What if all the clothes I wear ---------were dorky
What if I took acid and jerked off
Again and again because I'm quirky

Would you still believe in me?!
Would you still believe in me, my lord?!

What if I did something irrational
What if I fell for a fashion girl------real hard
What if she laid me to rest
And now she doesn't send her best---regards

Would you still believe in me?!
Would you still believe in me, my lord?!

Cause' now I feel I'm dyin'
And I just keep on tryin'
To rid myself of life and live through all this strife
And confusion cause' I have no wife

Somehow I know that you believe in me
Somehow I know that you conceived of me
Somehow I know that you believe in me, my Lord

I INTIMIDATE THE human race because
I shine like the sun.

WHAT IT IS TO BE Generation X
Is to be forgotten, looked down on and cast aside
Though the definition could conceivably be more complex
I'm mainly referring to our heroes who died

Kurt Cobain and Layne Staley
Have left behind a residue of human feelings
That our culture used to demonstrate daily
But have now been replaced with clones and money

Bad Religion and Pearl Jam
Still bark there objection to our social decline
Just another e mail spam
They too are washed away with the deleting tide

And Chris Cornell is still
And his impact superficial at best
Not by any fault of his
But because of the deficiency of the rest

A generation who saw
The dying of the Collective Soul
An age usurped by vacant lots
And hedonistic revelry extolled

Even Tupac, Snoop and Dre
Had a hint of righteous indignation
But the insect eyes of the artists today
Show nary a sign of even the basest revelation

America moving backward
In our foreign policy and at home
And living here is awkward
And unattached I roam

Generation X saw the demise
The next generation brought the rise

Of Godless good-looking ones and lies
Like a beast that quickly and sadly dies

Women who try to torture
Those who are allured by the illusion
Who they will dis for sure
For sharing in the pathological confusion

And so the last remaining humans with a soul
Did as all the enlightened ones have always done
They gave themselves to those who stole
And evaporated into the forgotten sun

WHAT MTV DESTROYED is irreplaceable now
What consumerism ruined is gone forever
What money hungry, clone robots decimated
Can never again be attained

Instead of thought provoking musical and visual expressions
By real artists with souls
There is a feeding frenzy for the last remaining tidbits of culture
Parasites with black eyes scouring the landscape

Instead of an open forum upon which American's could express themselves
There is instead a racket of movies, music and video games
And because Americans have chosen to worship money
Good art will forever be obscured, relegated, and under appreciated

There are only a few of us remaining
Standing firm against the tide of soullessness and parasitism
Like a scene from "Dawn of the Dead"
The world has been consumed by Godless, lifeless zombies with dollar signs in their eyes

WHAT RED ORB IS it that I see this night
Which doesn't twinkle yet shines true and steady
It must be Venus or Mars
Or perhaps another Greek god displayed in the Getty

Can it see the wrinkle in my love
That I have yet to fully iron out
Am I clearly disheveled from its perspective up above
Does it perceive how long I have been in drought

Climbing to the constellations
Past the temporality of these bodies
I read the golden compilations
And lend an ear to the masterful melodies

That bring color and ink to this climb
And delineate the tragic and heroic histories
And I write another seemingly meaningless rhyme
So I might pass along a bit of my own story

My quest for the heavens with the burden of my yoke
I unload some cargo each time I decide to not indulge
In some lustful endeavor or stifle myself in smoke
Or let my hatred grow or my fragile ego bulge

Peace is what I treasure now
No longer searching for constant stimuli
So long have I been face down on the ground
Tonight my inner gaze is upward to the starry sky

WHEN DOES THE LIGHT turn green
By turning red for good
When do I finally break free
When do I finally do what I should

As years pass by and the ivy grows heavy
Over the gate
I gaze and wonder if I shall soon be ready
Yet I wait

How stressed out do I have to get
How many uncomfortable fuck ups have to take place
Before I start what hasn't been started yet
The journey up to the garden of disciplined grace

All of my dreams are paralyzed within my head
Stuck stoned
All that I am to accomplish in this life before I'm dead
Postponed

What will I say to Jesus
When my time to face him comes
About the space between us
Before I'm tossed into those ovens

What of my talents, what of my gifts
Buried alive
Somehow the light snuck between the rifts
I've survived

But I feel myself reaching the end of God's mercy
Like a train coming to the end of the tracks
And that I've pushed him this far really hurts me
But the Prodigal Son eventually came back

WHEN I CAVE IN, to the same temptations of the past
Satan lashes at me in my thoughts and painful things occur to me
How many years I've languished in my pathetic sins
How little I've accomplished with my life

And then he reminds of how I was rejected from the start
How I played the part of a powerless rebel
How I continue to play the part of a slave to a financial system
How they didn't want me for sports, sex or poetry

And an all too familiar grief pervades my vessel
I look around at the society that progressed into plastic
And left me behind each step along the way
How agonizingly lonely, how devastatingly real

And entertainers are lauded beyond the sage
And contrivance is extolled beyond the truth
And millionaires with their moments in the sun
Join him in taunting me on this starless night

These are the necessary consequences for one who knows but doesn't go
The dream is obscured by the fresh sins I began my day with
Jesus, who rose from the dead, had the victory over Satan
And through prayer I shall remove the thorns that have strangled my fruit

WHEN I THINK BACK and add it all up
It's no wonder I'm fucked!
A young child, poisoned and corrupt
Then forced to move to a town that sucked

Hated in that town 'cause I didn't go to their church
Ostracized because I didn't do the right things
Drugs and sex I used to elude the hurt
And permanent damage is what these things bring

I'm so angry that I won't rescue my own soul
I can't believe my spirit has endured
Jerk off, get laid and smoke another bowl
And then hate myself for being impure

I see how the world is, turning its back on me
Poisoned and left to wrought in my wretched pathology
But when I finally climb out the world will see
That I've defied psychology and biology

When I think back on all the times I've masturbated you out of me
When I think back on the times I've cried, or merely died inside
It seems that you've taken a lot out on me, you've taken a lot out of me
My self-esteem was lied, my hands were tied, and I lost all my pride

Feeling inferior has sent me reeling this time, down and out of control
I just can't bring myself to suck it up sometimes
Sent to die on this lonely perch, abandoned to my anxious soul
Love is bound to be grueling climb

When "your anchor is up, you've been swept away"
And you've left home because you're bored and insatiable
And your reptilian skin makes you want to rewind the day
You wonder why the allure was so sensational

The cigarette, the sex, the drug that defiled you from within
Makes you sweat a little from the forehead even on a cold day
And just when your heavy hands are ready and willing to begin
A small voice inside of you is still begging you to stay

But we lie to ourselves for the millionth time
And give in like victims to the oldest trick in the book
We convince ourselves that it's all right
And our better angels beckon us but we refuse to look

Have a drink, have a smoke, buy a sack, get laid
We think we're keeping up with the tarnished Joneses
But this Jones leaves us broken and flayed
And showing our wretched and broken bones

But the hunger still remains like God's test for his elect
And the Satanic ego innate to the human thinks we need them
The sinful colors that stain all that's white and correct
Because black and white our heroes were able to blend

Jesus is so hard to follow really
Because he says love everyone
And sometimes compassion leaves us reeling
And feeling for those deprived of the sun

And we try to mold ourselves into those who can relate
To those down trodden ones who lie on the shore
And out of what is surely sin we create
A tether to those who have suffering in store

And as cool as it may seem to be Sublime or find Nirvana
In Eternal Truth these voices passed by the wayside
So smoke two joints in the morning and two at night if you wanna'
But don't forget why Bradley and Cobain sighed.

Whether you're good or bad, you're eternal
And whether you're alive or dead you exist
Whether the rules suit you or not, they apply
And whether you find Him or not, you may die

Only should the former be you're fate
You shall eat the proper Bread
And should this Bread be tasted
Our eternal soul is not wasted

And we can once again escape the lie
And we can once again reside on high
No suffering exists, only eternal bliss
And you only pity the fools that are still blind

WHO IS IT THAT SPEAKS to me, I thought sure I'd heard a voice
A whisper from within, but answering instead of inquiring
Is it only me in here? In this mind, in this body, in this soul?

I thought I heard her correct me from within
She told me love is more than an idea,
And I think it hurt her feelings that I called it that.

WIND LIKE GOD, you blow through this dark night
Wind like God you remain hidden from our sight
Wind like God we only see you're effects
Wind like God we perceive but don't detect

Wind like God is permeating all things
Wind like God we know but cannot see
Wind like God your power I behold
Wind like God, you're essence I extol

Wisdom comes in and sits with us on cold, dark nights, when we restrain ourselves enough for wisdom to begin to whisper itself through our clouds of delusion.

Surrendering ourselves to the night and allowing our eyes to begin purification and behold absolute truth, as valued by the ages.

Calming our longing souls with visions of trusting light and warming encouragement.

Stretching itself out along our journey, it climbs into its own space along each plane and resides there until we forget, only to remember again what you've always known.

Smelling each day and knowing the freshness of the vibrancy, receiving the day like a new emotion waiting to drive us forward, or calm us down.

Being still and letting the day take its course, following the footsteps of where your imagination has already taken you, the temple within your dreams, where we all realize the furthest truth, the truth that knows the absolute depth and the utmost height at once, encompassing both and bringing unfathomable balance and order to a chaotic and self-opposing universe.

Kiss her goodnight as she has longed with you, smile at the night and know that she will find forgiveness.

And learn from divine, poetic justice.

With regards to world affairs of this day
2003 or whatever,
Who cares when you're eternal but I have to say
We can't police the world forever.

Who are we to tell Iraq, this is how you'll be
We carved our nation
Who's to say our people are really free
In this present situation

Slaves we are to Capital, but yet it beat the Ruskies
And our money towers stand
I say we go have a few brewskies
And take a look at our own land

Those damn terrorists did bomb us
And that was fucked up
But do we dare call ourselves Christians
When we hold a bitter grudge

We built this city,
Not on rock and roll
We carved this city
And we sacrificed our soul!

May Jesus have pity!

Y<small>OU CAN CREATE</small> the sunset that you go off into
And no matter what anyone says, you can make it so
God only uses full vases, and what greater joy can there be than to be used by Him
And all things will come in time

YOU DIDN'T GO AND catch millionaireitis did you
An Axldemic, Matalli-plague is still upon us all
Pearl Jam Inc.
Kurt Cobain Enterprises
At least Greg Graffin is a professor
And he still moves you in the search for truth

Alanis caved into the puddle deep revolution
Jewel became Brittney Lite
Billy Joe started wearing eyeliner but his soul still yelps
Dave Mustaine rocked steady like the machine that he is
Passion can survive millionairedom

But it so seldom does
The soul gives way to worldliness
And stops screaming for liberation
Because you have settled into complacency
And no longer do you yearn

Real joy, real pain used to pulsate through them
But some of them have apparently succumbed to the prevailing epidemic
Bob Dylan kept his soul fire burning
Bob Marley the same
And Type O Negative manage to stir the soul

After years of money and fame
Paul McCartney still preaches love
And Bono and Ringo are still on board
Even if it tastes like a rice cake sometimes
The ingredients are still wholesome

I have to thank the good lord that I wasn't chosen
And put to the test before I was ready
I follow my quite spirit, keeping myself beneath my coat
I'll do my humble penance
Traffic jams, corporate job, financial stress

I'd rather have my soul than be a star

You ever watch an old movie and just think
That was the beginning of two dimensionality
That was the beginning of screens
We want to watch the world.

People used to use their brains and have values
People used to tell stories and read books
People were assessed by their merits rather that their anatomy
There wasn't all this emphasis on sports and looks

And isn't it interesting that the two biggest wars in world history took place after movies were invented.
And then TV led us into Vietnam
And now computers are taking us into oblivion
More immediacy, more artifice, more My Space

And personal pages, and isolated lives
Lonely car rides, against the other satellites
Post Modernism, fragmentation, coldness and hate
And superficial crap like expensive, loveless weddings

Bridzillas represents the epitome of shallow artifice
Huge emphasis placed on a ceremony and none placed on love
I can feel how badly all the people want to be in the spotlight
The envy of all the other godless clones who yearn to be witnessed

They want so bad to be seen, captivating the collective attention with immediate artifice
An image that fools the drones into believing they have succeeded at something
But all that they have accomplished is getting completely lost in the abyss
And become the target for those who love to tell the tale of the fall

Despite the obvious desolation and pathology of Anna Nichole, Brittney and their ilk
They attract a horde of young whores, out to get dick, pussy and a beamer
And now every young dude is emulating some star of stage and screen
An athlete or an artist, an image that calls to their warped minds

But I will be on the front lines of the revolution, the reckoning
When America comes back into its heart, beneath the black
Time will bring it all back to me, the one who stayed still
And I will right that which was led astray with black and white movies in the twenties

I BELIEVE IN ENTROPY, the return, the restoration
This well documented age will be forgotten
As the wisdom of those in the future learn the lessons of us
And appreciate people, and seek internal gratification

When will our stories and movies tell us something about the inside
When will our idols seek inner peace, when will we extol compassion
When will we live as one, and not against each other in feats of pride
When will we leave the narrative on the screen and live our lives out here on the inside

You ask me how I can be so sure
That Christ is the truth
And I say let's call it faith

Besides
Who wants to live in a world of certainty
Life by definition is not sure
Thus life may cease at any time, for anyone
And were it not that way, existence would be futile

THANK YOU MY gracious Christ
For not allowing me to neglect myself
To the point of destruction
So that I might now appreciate
The beauty and awe of your perfection

Timing is essential, and it is everything!
And yours is always perfect
There is a steady consciousness
 That is in perfect harmony with
 That which is beyond time

The time for everything comes
We need only await the One who knows best
For He is the one that will set Time
And to resist is futile and tragic
For one would neglect such magic

ABOUT THE AUTHOR

THE AUTHOR HAS A BACHELORS DEGREE in Literature and Film and Digital Media from the University of Califonia at Santa Cruz. He has been writing poetry since he was 18 years old and writes about his spiritual journey through life but also comments on cultural and political circumstances in the modern world.

Printed in the United States
By Bookmasters